D0456007

Driven

*Reflections on love, career,
and the pursuit of happiness*

Venise Berry

Published by BerryBooks, LLC
an imprint of Jewell Jordan Publishing LLC

~~~~~~

Each essay is written from the author's experience. Most names, locations and identifying details have been changed for privacy purposes. Some liberties have also been taken concerning chronological order.

~~~~~~

Also by Venise Berry

So Good: An African American Love Story

All of Me: A Voluptuous Tale

Colored Sugar Water

The 50 Most Influential Black Films
(with S. Torriano Berry)

*The Historical Dictionary of African
American Cinema*
(with S. Torriano Berry)

Mediated Messages: Issues in African American Culture
(with Carmen Manning-Miller)

*Black Culture and Experience:
Contemporary Issues*
(with Anita Fleming-Ryfe and ayo dayo)

Printed in the United States of America.
10 9 8 7 6 5 4 3 2 1

Cover designed by Venise Berry
Cover drawing by William Beard

Library of Congress
PCN: 2018951284

Published by BerryBooks, LLC
an imprint of Jewell Jordan Publishing, LLC

For more information contact:
Jewell Jordan Publishing, LLC
1205 South Air Depot Blvd. Suite 153
Midwest City, Oklahoma 73110

stephana@jewelljordanpublishing.com

Hardcover ISBN: 978-0-9778418-0-6
Paperback ISBN: 978-0-9778418-1-3
Ebook ISBN: 978-0-9778418-2-0

~~~~~~

Acknowledgements

My Lord and Savior Jesus Christ is always the first on my list. He has brought me a mighty long way.

My family is my inspiration and my friends are my motivation for writing these essays. I love all of you very much!

I'm thankful for the men in my life who have loved me and taught me some very valuable lessons about relationships.

I appreciate the faith that my publisher Stephana Colbert of Jewell Jordan Publishing has in this work.

And I can't forget women, especially my African American sisters who are holding on to their dream of having a good man and maintaining a career at the same time. Good luck and God bless!

Table of Contents

Baby Boomers   9

What Do You Believe?
Fifty/Fifty   13
The "L" Word   16
Saints and Sinners   19
Knock on Wood   23
The Book of Job   28
Valentine's Day   32
A Hopeful Romantic   35

We Are Family
A Good Man   39
Blue Moon   43
Purple Rain   47
Deal or No Deal   51
Hoochies, Hotties, and Hoes   54
Late Bloomers   58

Kindred Spirits
Good Dick   63
What's Love Got to Do With It?   65
Age Versus Beauty   69
From Fact to Fiction   73
Janet Jackson – Control   76
Animal Crackers   79
Playin' the Game   82
Angry Black Women   84

It's Raining Men

Driven 89
Heaven Must be Like This 91
The Engagement Ring 94
My Baby's Daddy 99
A Train Ride to Boston 103
Tired Black Men 105
Peace My Sister 108
SweetChocolate 112

Life Goes On

Black Love in a Big White House 116
My Heavenly Bed 121
Jouissance 124
Proverbial Wisdom 129
Cruisin' 133
Live Long and Prosper 137
God is Love 144
Letting Go 148
A Life Worth Living 151

Works Cited 157
Biography 171

~~~~~~

Baby Boomers

I remember the first AARP newsletter I pulled out of my mailbox. I frowned and mumbled out loud, "What the hell are they sending me this for?" Even though I was old enough to be called a senior citizen, I didn't look like one, I didn't feel like one, and I refused to be called one. Fifty-years-old was still the prime of life. As a matter of fact, I had just watched a segment on *Good Morning America* where they declared that fifty was the new thirty citing Oprah Winfrey and Christie Brinkley as examples. Both are baby boomers like me.

Fighting against slavery, segregation, and discrimination African Americans dreamed of an equal America. Not long after the Civil Rights Movement emerged, women also demanded more rights in this country. According to a 2015 U.S. Census Bureau report, African Americans represent a little over twenty-five percent of the baby boomers and women make up more than fifty percent of that generation.

I was born a baby boomer in 1955. I'm an African American and a woman. So, I absorbed a double dose of the desire for more: more opportunities, more power, more happiness, more respect, and more love.

At eight-years-old, I knew that something big was happening when Dr. Martin Luther King Jr. gave his "I Have a Dream Speech" during the 1963 March on Washington. And, at thirteen-years-old, I remember news reports about protests against the Miss America Pageant where feminists wrote "freedom" on trash barrels then filled them with bras, false eyelashes, mops, pots and pans, high heels, curlers, and girdles. They planned to burn everything, but unfortunately, the police would not allow them to start a fire in the city.

My generation, the baby boomers, were raised to be different. As a woman, the stereotype of the subservient, weaker sex, born to cook, clean and have babies was not the path that I chose to pursue. As an African American, the stereotype of being inferior, lazy, unintelligent, and unsuccessful was another path I did not accept. I pursued my education, found my passion, and lived my dream. I was raised to believe I could have it all.

I became one of those bra-burning, pants-wearing, education-getting, money-making, opinion-having, sex-enjoying, career-focused Black women who decided to live life and live it abundantly with or without a man. I learned a very important lesson over the years. Even though I love men, especially Black men, I have to love myself more.

Like many career women, I flew through my twenties and thirties and forties, but fifty brought everything to a sudden stop. My fiftieth birthday was like a thief that snuck up behind me, held a gun to my head, and demanded my soul. That milestone triggered a deep longing to better understand the choices I made in my life.

Now don't get it twisted, I have no regrets. I'm a mother and a daughter and a friend and a lover, and a child of God. My life has been, and is still very good.

Yet, I have to admit that there is something missing. Even though I know the elusive fairy tale doesn't really exist, there are moments when I yearn for the one thing that I've never had – marriage. I've never worn the long white gown or said "I do" or promised to share my life till death do us part.

These essays are an exploration of my journey. An effort to understand the choices I made. The structure of this book is not in the traditional arc of moving from childhood to adulthood. Instead, I wrote each essay looking for the answer to one important question - Why don't I have it all?

Answering this question meant examining my beliefs about my career and relationships. I had to look at how family and friends have influenced me. I wanted to evaluate the decisions I made concerning the men in my life. Finally, I needed to explore the broader ideas and experiences that have made this journey worthwhile.

What Do You Believe?

~~~~~

*"Whatever we believe about ourselves
and our ability comes true for us."*

Susan L. Taylor

~~~~~~

Fifty/Fifty

Society pushes marriage like a drug dealer pushes crack. Yet, fifty percent of marriages end in divorce, and many young people are marrying much later in life, if at all. So, what happened to the real love, true love, magical love that we've all been co-erced into dreaming about? How did it turn into this vicious cycle of finding happiness and comfort with Prince Charming one day, then waking up in misery the next day with a cold, croaking frog?

In my first novel, *So Good: An African American Love Story,* one of the main characters Danielle explains a theory she developed about love called the "Shit-Tolerance Theory." It says that relationships are based on how much shit one person is will-ing to take from another person. In other words, for a relationship to work each person has to determine his or her own shit-tolerance level and then find someone who doesn't cross the line. And it is important to remember that shit-tolerance levels can change over time. This is a theory that I live by. The older I get the less shit I'm willing to put up with.

Think about it, some people have really high shit-tolerance levels and others not so high. Former First Lady Hillary Clinton stayed with her husband, former President Bill Clinton after he lied about having sexual relations with Monica Lewinsky in the oval office, so her shit-tolerance level has to be off the charts. She was able to hold it together while he continued to govern the country. But once they left the White House, maybe during a visit to Arkansas, I hope she took Bill out back to the woodshed and gave him the ass-whoopin' he deserved.

On the other side, Lorena Bobbitt obviously had a much lower shit-tolerance level when it came to infidelity and abuse from her husband, John Wayne. She grabbed a knife, cut off his penis and ran out of the house. According to news reports, Lorena jumped in the car still holding the penis in her hand until several miles down the road when she flung it out of the window. As a side note, somehow it was miraculously found and doctors sewed it back on. John Wayne Bobbitt later took advantage of his adversity starring in a fairly successful porno movie called, *Frankenpenis*.

Anyway, when it comes to taking shit, everybody has limits and we all need to know what our limits are. Apparently, Elin Nordegren didn't simply walk out the door when she found out about Tiger Wood's serial infidelity. She went after him with one of his own golf clubs. And we can't forget the NASA astronaut who, according to police reports, drove almost a thousand miles to confront her competition wearing an adult diaper, so that she wouldn't have to stop to use the bathroom.

The bottom line is obvious: shit stinks. As women get older, they sometimes get more desperate. Our friends and families start to ask irritating questions about the last dud-of-a-boyfriend we had, or they feel it is their duty to remind us of the optimum time for baby making. We begin to worry that maybe there's no one around the corner, hold our nose, and settle. A few years later we find ourselves in the middle of a divorce wondering what happened.

It is also a possibility that our "Shit-Tolerance" level can become warped. I heard a story about a woman who decided she was going to marry a married man. They had been in an affair for several years and she was in love. Convinced that he would leave his wife, she started to plan a wedding. She bought the ring, set a date, found a venue, picked out her dress, and sent out the invitations. A number of folks showed up, but he didn't. I don't know how much that married man supported her delusion. Maybe he let her believe she had a chance when she didn't. Maybe he wanted to leave his wife, but couldn't. No matter how it happened, the fact that she planned the wedding without seeing divorce papers means her "Shit Tolerance" level was definitely warped.

I think, as a career woman, it's hard to make the commitment when fifty/fifty is the best you can hope for. A study at the University of Calgary found that marriage for men was a more positive experience, while for women it had a greater potential to bring on depression. Some women were depressed because it was not going the way they hoped it would go, and others were depressed because he was not who they thought he should be.

For many career women fifty/fifty is a problem. For example, I need a certain kind of man. Some say I've set the bar too high and there is no way any man can jump over it. But, I've watched many women place the bar too low and the man does nothing but step over it. A man should add value to my life. He should be somebody who can fill in the gaps. Somebody I can depend on. Somebody who has my back. And, together we should be able to create a happy and healthy relationship where we are both appreciated, supported, and loved.

Venise Berry

~~~~~~

The "L" Word

Sometimes I think the next revolution for women should be the elimination of the "L" word from our vocabularies. Now I know that losing the word "love" is not as easy as it sounds, but in my opinion, the "L" word is just as toxic for women as the "N" word is for African Americans. Too many women get caught up in that word and lose sight of the real goal.

The first time I tried, I wrote the word down on a piece of paper, set it on the grill, and watched it burn. A few months later, I met somebody interesting, and after dating for almost a year that relationship failed. I wrote the word on another piece of paper, went out on my upstairs deck, ripped that piece of paper into tiny little pieces, and watched them blow away with the autumn breeze. Once, while on vacation in Florida, in between relationships I used a marker to write the word on a small rock, and then threw that rock as far as I could into the Atlantic Ocean. I actually held out for several years that time.

Almost every woman I know has one "lost-a-man-by-say-ing-the-L-word story." A neighbor in Texas told me about a guy she was seeing who had a panic attack whenever he heard the "L" word. He acted as if her next step would be to chain him up in the basement and turn him into her sex slave. A friend living in Illinois said she mentioned the "L" word to one boyfriend and he ran so fast he eventually started winning marathons.

Another friend in California told me she jokingly said those three little words, "I love you," and the guy she was dating must have joined the witness protection program because he literally disappeared. His phone number was suddenly disconnected, and when she stopped by his apartment a couple of weeks later he had moved out. There was even a married woman from Georgia who told me that she had been married to her husband for almost twenty years, but he still sweated and shook like a drug addict in detox whenever he had to say those words.

I honestly don't get it. You meet an interesting man. Get to know him. Laugh easily together. Fantasize about the future. Connect in powerful and passionate ways. Then, in that one moment, those words are spoken, and it's over.

The word "love" means different things to different people. That's primarily why it's a hard concept for both men and women to deal with. You can love having someone in your life, but it doesn't mean you want him or her to move into your house. You can love the way someone makes you laugh, but it doesn't mean you want to sponsor his or her comedy career. You can love making love with somebody, but it doesn't mean your vibrator can't do the job when he's not around.

Actually when you think about it, the "L" word is really not as important as women make it out to be. After fifty years, the one thing I know for sure is that talk is cheap. Men say a lot of things, but love is really about what a man does. Admit it, even when a man tells you that he loves you, you still wonder. How much does he love me? Is he serious? What does he really mean when he says he loves me? Plus, we all know some men will say the words, then go on to do whatever with whomever.

So, how do we deal with the "L" word? I've thought about this a lot. Eventually, coming up with an adaptation of the Alcoholics Anonymous Twelve-Step program. This would be a six-step Love Anonymous program. I hope to see Love Anonymous groups created across the country where women can come together and help keep each other on track.

The six steps are:

1. We must admit that we are powerless over love and that our relationships are unmanageable.
2. We must believe that we need a Power (God) greater than ourselves to restore stability in our relationships.
3. We must take a thorough inventory of our own actions and attitudes concerning love in past relationships, those where we were right and those where we were wrong.
4. We must make a list of the people to whom we have said the "L" word, but they didn't respond appropriately and forgive them.
5. We must make a list of people who have said the "L" word to us, but didn't mean it, and forgive them.
6. We must pray for the will and the power to create more positive relationships by eliminating the confusion and problems caused by the "L" word.

Just like the Alcoholics Anonymous Twelve Step Program can help a recovering alcoholic, I'm hoping these six steps can help recovering lovesick women finally get a grip.

~~~~~~

Saints and Sinners

Donnie McClurkin's song *We Fall Down* says, "A saint is just a sinner who fell down and got back up." I think about this song almost every Sunday in church recognizing the serious imbalance between Christian single women and Christian single men. Many black churches consist of mainly couples and single women. Every now and then a single man might show up and when he does he is golden.

One particular day after church I remember watching five single young ladies gathered around one single young man, each vying for his attention. For single Christian women the options are limited and somehow they have to navigate the disparity.

Imagine author, feminist, and social activist bell hooks versus educational consultant and author Dr. Jawanza Kunjufu in a rhetorical boxing match. They are discussing the importance of love, sex, and marriage. I watched this ideological battle late one night on television. When the metaphorical bell rang the interview began. Dr. Kunjufu led with a quick left hook arguing that because love-making is a key principle in Christianity, in order to be right with God, Christian people should only participate when they are married. The challenger bell hooks stepped back, and let go of a right uppercut asking, "But as a single woman, don't I deserve love too?" Ding, Ding, Ding, as far as I was concerned it was a knockout. The fight was over.

Don't get me wrong, I understand that marriage is the ultimate goal and it should be the primary purpose of any relationship, but marriage takes two people. How many times have you thought that he was "Mr. Do Right" only to later realize he was "Mr. So Wrong?"

If single women accept the fact that they must be married to experience love and sex it can bring about serious problems. For example, maybe the woman jumps into marriage too soon and it doesn't work out. Or, maybe if the idea is taken to the extreme, a woman who wants love and sex badly enough might decide to break up somebody else's marriage so that she can have him for herself. There is also the woman who stays in an unhealthy marriage dealing with issues of depression, adultery, domestic violence, or all of the above because she believes that is the only way.

After going through a very difficult divorce, a colleague once warned me to be careful of the fairy tale. When I close my eyes I can still see Sheila's sad, puffy eyes, and chewed-up bottom lip. She and her husband seemed like the perfect couple, attentive to each other and visibly in love. Then one day without warning, for those of us on the outside, he moved out of their custom-built home and into the apartment of his new woman.

Sometimes relationships look good on the outside because people only show you what they want you to see. Living in that relationship on a daily basis is the only way to understand the reality. It is hard to make the ultimate commitment to another human being, and even harder once you've made that commitment to follow through. You bicker over silly things like he forgets to put the toilet seat down or she doesn't make up the bed when she was the last one in it.

A rumor spread through the office that Sheila's seven-year relationship with her husband had started almost the same way it ended. They, apparently, met at a party and more than one person in attendance described the heat between them as combustible. A little more than a year later, he moved in with Sheila and filed for divorce from his first wife. They were married almost a year after that.

Now rational thought should suggest that if he would leave his first wife for you, he might leave you for another woman. But rational thought is pushed to the side when passion, excitement, and hope take over. We think, "Of course he loves me. He is leaving his wife for me. I'm the one he wants to be with."

Sheila knew how he treated his first wife. He played around on her, used her, disrespected her, and then dumped her. But Sheila believed that the other woman was the problem and she was the solution. That's what we do, right? We think that we can make the difference.

But I digress. How do we solve the problem concerning single, Christian women who want to be loved? First, it is important to remember that being single does not mean we are alone. And second, we must understand that God is love. Marriage cannot be the difference between love and sex because there are too many marriages that lack the main ingredient, love.

Love is about two people connecting with each other to experience parts of each other that are sacred. There is a bond that brings with it longing and passion and desire. Sex, as good as it may feel at the moment, may not have that same bond ultimately leaving you unfulfilled and unsatisfied.

In the 21st century as women demand more dignity and respect, it is important to note that so many women in the *Bible* are treated poorly. Eve was created by God to be a helper for Adam. In Genesis, Eve is blamed for his choice and they are banished from Eden. In 1 Corinthians, females are considered inferior, told to be silent in the church, and obedient to man. The book of Judges talks about a woman who is gang raped then cut into pieces by her husband and spread across Israel. Finally, King David in Exodus took hundreds of wives and concubines because he saw women as slaves and sex objects.

I have heard many Christian women say that they are waiting and praying for their Boaz. Boaz is a wealthy landowner who notices poverty-stricken Ruth in his fields searching for leftover grain from the harvest. He orders his workers to leave more grain for Ruth and eventually takes her as his wife. Some argue that the story of Ruth and Boaz is not really about love between the two of them. When Ruth chooses to stay with Naomi, they declare their love for the God of Israel and both return to Bethlehem. So, Ruth marries Boaz for protection and stability. And, as a distant relative of Naomi, Boaz sees his union with Ruth as a duty to support both women.

If love is about intimacy, then sex alone is not enough. Sex cannot give ultimate fulfillment because to be fulfilled a woman needs to be valued and appreciated. Sex cannot give ultimate satisfaction because to be satisfied she must experience joy and gratification. In other words, marriage may not be the answer even if it is the goal.

What I have learned on my journey is that I matter. What I want is important. How I feel is relevant. And, a relationship that takes one or all of those elements away is not about love. As a single Christian woman bell hook's question is real for me, "Don't I deserve love too?" Don't I deserve to experience a heated touch, a soft kiss, and the ecstasy of entangled passion?

Whenever Donnie McClurkin sings, "A saint is just a sinner who falls down and gets back up," I think been there, done that.

~~~~~

Knock on Wood

I am a Christian. I have been baptized. I believe in the power of prayer. I believe that Jesus died on the cross to save my soul. Those incidents that some people call luck or chance or miracles, I call God's blessings. But sometimes I knock on wood, cross my fingers, or make a wish. These acts are not separate from my connection with God. He speaks to us in many different ways and in my heart everything leads back to Him.

Years ago, I picked up a wonderful book called *Knock on Wood and Other Superstitions*. In this book, Carole Potter includes the history behind many of our most prominent superstitions. For example, she suggests that some people believed that evil spirits could get caught in a knot and that belief was responsible for the design of the clerical collar replacing the tie. The word bride comes from the name for a cook in old English. Therefore, a woman cooking equals bride. She also discusses how daisies have been called the smile of God because the white petals open during the day and close at nightfall.

Potter's book describes the superstition of knocking on wood. She says when people knock on wood they are making sure something bad doesn't happen. The Druids believed that gods lived in trees, so they would knock on the bark to ask a favor then come back later and knock again to say thanks if the favor was granted. Potter added that knocking on wood has also been connected to bragging. In some cultures, bragging is said to bring forth jealous spirits, so to avoid being punished for bragging people would knock on wood.

As a Christian, my life is shaped by my positive relationship with God, but superstition, other religions, and spirituality are still fascinating to me. I've been to a palm reader, a past-life hypnotist, played with an Ouija Board, and had my future illustrated by Tarot cards. I know there are some Christians that see these things as evil. I believe God is everywhere, so I don't have to be afraid. In the Bible, magicians, enchanters, sorcerers, mediums, and fortune tellers are called false prophets that we should not follow. I believe God is in control, so my faith allows me to understand without following.

Is it wrong that I enjoy reading my horoscope in the newspaper or a monthly magazine? Horoscopes are based on the earth, sun, moon, and stars. These are all God's creations. There is a song by gospel singer Mandisa called "God Speaking." The lyrics suggest that there are many things we can't explain such as unexpected death or the beauty of a sunrise. Mandisa asks "What if God is speaking to us through those situations?" I believe God does speak through a variety of situations, so He could send me a message in my horoscope.

Astrological signs actually serve another purpose. They are interesting as broad-based personality charts. Different signs tend to display certain characteristics. For example, I'm a Libra and there are three things that seem to be true about all Libras. First, peace is essential. Libras will do whatever they have to do to avoid unnecessary conflict. We don't like to fight, however, if backed into a corner we will defend ourselves. Second, Libras strive for balance in their lives. The symbol for Libra is the scale of justice representing balance. So when a Libra is off-balance it feels like our whole world is in turmoil. Third, Libras are in love with love. Love is joy. Love is peace. Love is beauty. Love is life. We need love like a doctor needs sick patients, like a fish needs water, or like a tree needs the soil.

All signs have one or more prominent characteristics. Scorpios seem to thrive on drama. They are very demanding and controlling. Virgos are wishy-washy. They are critical of others while ignoring their own flaws. Cancers are sensitive and moody. They are very affectionate, but the pendulum swings both ways. The major focus for a Gemini is communication. Yet, they can easily shift from hot to cold, curious to bored or faithful to unfaithful.

I explored spirituality in my third novel, *Colored Sugar Water.* The main character Lucy believes in everything from fortune telling and healing to Christianity and Voodoo. Her best friend Adel was raised in a family that was not religious, so she doesn't know what to believe. Both characters take different spiritual journeys to find their faith.

During my research for *Colored Sugar Water,* I read about different religions like Christianity, Voodoo, Judaism, and Buddhism. I talked to several preachers about how they got the call to preach, and I met the coordinator of a psychic hot line who invited me to her annual psychic conference in Pittsburg. I also talked with a healer in Louisiana about what she called her magical gifts. My research while writing this book enabled me to explore my own notions about God, religion, and spirituality. Writing *Colored Sugar Water* brought me closer to my own walk with Jesus.

For example, I think everyone has a sixth sense, and if you are a child of God, I believe that sixth sense is God speaking. Unfortunately, a lot of people don't pay attention to their sixth sense. When I meet someone who I automatically don't like or don't trust, that's my sixth sense at work. I acknowledge that God is telling me to stay away. When I meet someone and feel like I've known them all of my life, that's God guiding me too.

I didn't always pay attention to my sixth sense. When I was still in high school, I missed my bus one morning and started walking. While waiting at a corner for the stoplight to change, a red Mercury Comet pulled up next to me. A young white guy leaned over and spoke to me through the open passenger window.

"Hey, don't you go to Tech High?" He asked.

I nodded and the light changed, so I started to walk again. He crossed the street and slowed down on the other side waiting for me to catch up. "I'm on my way to Tech. You want a ride?" He offered.

Now my sixth sense warned me not to get into the car. I had never seen this man at Tech, but I didn't know a lot of the white kids at the school, so he could be telling the truth. Plus, if I had a ride I could get to school on time. And just like that I did something really stupid. I ignored my sixth sense, God's guidance, and got into his car.

I regretted my decision as soon as the door shut. The guy drove forward and I sat stiffly in the passenger seat. I started to think about what I might do if he turned out to be a psycho killer. This was in the early seventies, so cars did not have electric locks back then. I checked to make sure my door was unlocked. While the car continued down the street, I watched him closely, along with the passing street signs.

"So what year are you?" He asked, suddenly breaking the tense silence between us.

"I'm a sophomore."

He smiled. "I'm a senior. This is my last year. Thank God."

I swallowed. He said "Thank God" maybe that is a good sign. Iowa doesn't have a lot of crime like major cities, so growing up in Iowa makes people more trusting.

I took a good look at his face in case I had to identify him to the police later. He basically looked like an average white guy, brown hair, brown eyes, maybe six feet tall, and really thin. He had a cross tattooed on the back of his right hand. I have to admit when I saw the cross I felt better too. If he knew God, he should also know the sixth commandment "Thou shall not kill."

"Today's my birthday," he announced.

"Happy birthday," I replied. It was May 22nd. I made a quick calculation in my head. He was a Gemini and they often have dual personalities. He could be a Dr. Jekyll and Mr. Hyde character.

"I think I'm going to see a movie tonight. You like movies?" He asked.

I nodded my head thinking it was a strange question. Didn't

everybody like movies?

He continued, "What kind of movies do you like?"

I shrugged. "I saw *The Omega Man* recently with Charlton Heston. It was pretty good."

"I saw that, too. I liked it. I might go see *Escape from the Planet of the Apes*."

Even though he hadn't done anything wrong I was still very uncomfortable. I scooted closer to the door. His conversation seemed pretty normal and we were heading toward the school, but my sixth sense was screaming now. Something just wasn't right. I stayed in alert mode. I crossed my fingers and said a quick prayer. "Please God keep me safe, Amen."

"What about a favorite class?" He asked as we stopped at a red light.

"I'm in Radio, TV and Film."

"Oh, you're going to be on TV? You're pretty. You should be on TV."

I flashed a quick smile. "Thanks."

"You dress nice, too," he added.

We were still stopped at the light when he reached over, pretending to feel the texture of my blue, silk blouse. "What kind of material is that?"

He did not stop at feeling the material. Suddenly, he was touching my breast. I panicked. Just as the light turned green, but before he could take off, I threw open the car door, jumped out, and started running. A few blocks down the street, I ducked into a grocery store and used the pay phone to call my mother. I told her I had missed my bus. She picked me up.

This is the first time I've ever told anyone what happened that day because I felt stupid. I knew better than to get into that car. They say God protects babies and fools. We all have a sixth sense. I started paying more attention after that and as a result I have experienced God at work in my life many times.

Over the next week, I looked closely at every white male face I passed in the halls at Tech High, but I never saw him again. Thank God and knock on wood.

~~~~~~

The Book of Job

In the Old Testament of the *Bible*, Job was a rich man with everything he wanted in life, materially and spiritually, until Satan and God used him in a test. God trusted the strength of Job's faith so much that he allowed Satan to murder Job's children, destroy his crops, kill his animals, and inflict him with disease and pain. Most of Job's friends turned on him, and his wife encouraged him to curse the Lord.

Through it all Job refused to give in. He kept his faith. He believed in God's grace and trusted His love. So after Job had endured all of Satan's torture, God claimed victory. He gave Job a new life: a second family, good health, more wealth, and unspeakable joy. For my mom, the basic question from the story of Job is why would God be so mean? He allowed Job to suffer just to prove a point. But for me the story of Job raises a different question. What is it like to have a faith so strong that absolutely nothing can break it?

They say the Lord doesn't give you more than you can bare, but if I'm honest I have to admit that my faith is often challenged, especially when it comes to relationships. I know God answers prayers. He has brought me a mighty long way. But my prayers for him to send me the man of my dreams have not been answered yet.

Sometimes career women choose to be married or in a relationship because they are tired of the alternative, being alone. Maybe that's what we need to think about up front, so that we don't have to question our sanity after we ignore the red flags. He may seem like the answer to our prayers in the beginning. We want to believe that this time, this man is the right one. But when doubt crashes through the soul like a heavy rock through water the pain can't be ignored.

For many career-minded, independent Black women who have never been married or even those who have had the fantasy for a while and lost it, faith is fickle. As we get older, and hopefully wiser, we try to believe that the next relationship will be better. The next one will be different. The next one will be "the one."

I haven't had everything taken from me like Job. As a matter of fact, God has been very good to me in most areas of my life. But, the pain and sadness that comes from a broken relationship does weaken my faith. When I was younger I was able to brush off the sadness in a few weeks and get right back out there. But, now that I'm older it takes much longer to filter through the damage and restore my confidence.

Did you know that human beings could, literally, die of a broken heart? I didn't know that until I read an article in my favorite magazine, *Psychology Today*. They called it "broken heart syndrome." There is apparently a serious connection between the long-term depression and stress from a breakup and an increase in the risk of heart disease. Research has found that this powerful link between your emotional well-being and how your heart functions can literally cause a heart attack. That's an important consideration when black women are dying of heart attacks at a higher rate than any other group, according to a 2017 report by the Center for Disease Control and Prevention.

I have had to learn to protect my heart. Many of us have turned ourselves into well-trained soldiers placed carefully on the battlefield. We wear bulletproof vests to protect our hearts because when the shit starts flying through the air like bullets, we may not be able to get out of the way.

As an independent career woman, I have spent most of my life taking care of myself. It would be nice to turn things over to a man, but it's just not that easy. People tell me when real love comes along I will change. But, to be honest, I'm not sure I even believe in real love any more. At least, not the love we see in the movies. The kind that tickles hearts and tingles toes. I used to believe. But, at this point in my life when I think of love, I think of a cute, little puppy who even after you train him to go outside to do his business still shits on the floor, and you have to clean it up.

I know I can change if I want to. I once dated someone who was very old fashioned. He wanted to open doors and pull out chairs for me. He would actually get upset if I forgot and did those things for myself. I worked hard to reprogram my mind, trying to remember to let him do things like that for me. Of course, as soon as I began to get comfortable with the change he was gone.

Job's experience is not only a testimony to his faith, but to his strength. If black women have one claim to fame it is that we are strong. Through all of the trials and tribulations we keep moving forward. I refuse to be one of those women who hold on to a man, not because I really want him, but because I don't want to be alone.

Research on the optimum time to find a husband is contradictory. Society is changing, and more women are marrying later in life after building their careers. An article in the *Los Angeles Times* suggests that women are missing out on the prime marriage candidates in college. At the same time, a *Women's Health* article warns that college has become a hook up culture and therefore not good hunting ground for a lifetime commitment.

Even though career women don't have the same extreme challenges as Job, looking for love in this confusing world is a true test of faith for many. Especially as the acceptable male dating/ marrying pool continues to get smaller. In the African American community, we have all heard about the dismal state of educated and accomplished black men available for educated and accomplished black women. The numbers are low because of issues like drugs, the prison system, and men who are gay or on the down low. The PEW Research Center also reports that black men are twice as likely as black women to choose someone outside of their race to marry. Although things are changing, for many African American women crossing over the color line remains more difficult and nobody seems to know why.

I have mature, single, career oriented friends all across the country with faith, but they are still having trouble finding the right man. And, if I take a good look at my married friends maybe they have faith in their relationships, but there's nobody I would want to trade places with. I don't know anyone who would disagree with the fact that finding "the right man" is hard and keeping him is even harder.

I admire Job's faith. I strive to build my faith each day so that, like Job, I can believe no matter what. But, one of my favorite *Bible* verses is Mark 9:24: "Lord I believe; help my unbelief."

~~~~~~

Valentine's Day

It was Valentine's Day. I heard a knock on my office door and said, "Come in." I was very surprised to see a delivery guy with a large bouquet of flowers in his arms. The flowers were beautiful, a mixture of bright colors and sharp textures. I smiled. I wasn't dating anyone at the time, so I wondered who might have sent them. I let my imagination take over, thinking maybe my last boyfriend finally realized what he lost or maybe it was a secret admirer, somebody new.

The delivery guy smiled back and asked, "Mrs. Rodriguez?"

My face dropped. I pointed and replied, "Two doors down the hall."

In the third century A.D., Emperor Claudius II decided that his soldiers should not marry because they would be stronger in battle without wives and families to worry about. This is the legend of Saint Valentine, a romantic priest who secretly continued to marry young soldiers to the women they loved until he was caught and arrested. While in prison, Valentine sent a letter to his own love, a young blind girl. That letter is said to be the first valentine and that priest is considered the patron saint of lovers.

Valentine's Day is probably the one day out of the year that creates an abundance of conflicting and exasperating feelings among single women. If we were to be honest, we'd admit that this day makes us anxious, angry, insecure, sad, and maybe even desperate. This can happen whether we have someone in our life or not.

Why? Because so many of us don't really know what love is. C. S. Lewis in his book *The Four Loves* identifies four specific types of love and explains how they often get jumbled up in our heads. The first type is "charity." This is our love for humanity and for ourselves. It is like the love of God for his people. Lewis says this kind of love should manifest itself in everything we do as children of God.

The second love Lewis calls "affection" and suggests that it's a natural and familiar connection between two souls. Affection involves an attentive hug or a kiss on the cheek. It is very different from the hug or kiss we would get from a lover. Unfortunately, we sometimes mistake charity for affection.

According to Lewis, "friendship" relates to how much we care about others. It presents a deeper communal kind of love without the romantic interest. Friendship and affection can be confusing as well. A kiss or hug in friendship can also lead to other types of love depending on the energy and connection between both parties.

The fourth type of love is a merger of two ideas: full-blown romantic love and sex. Lewis suggests that love "Eros" and sexual desire "Venus" usually come together. He argues that they both involve touch, which adds power.

The lines between love and sex are definitely blurred today. As I discussed earlier in the "Saints and Sinners" essay, how many of us know the difference between a basic physical release like two people who are simply enjoying each other sexually, and a powerful, spiritual bond that links a couple together for the rest of their lives?

Flipping through the television channels late one night, I stopped when I heard an expert say: "...sex changes every thing!" I don't remember who the expert was or the name of the interview show, but I remember how she went on to describe the psychological dilemma that often occurs after a couple has had sex or makes love for the first time.

The expert explained that when a man meets a woman that he likes his focus, for the most part, is getting her into bed. He is probably not thinking about the long term or the real relationship potential. The expert continued from the woman's perspective suggesting that from the moment they met the woman was thinking about the possibility of a long-term relationship, maybe even hoping for marriage.

During the interview, the expert went on to discussed how many women need to believe that their connection with a man has lasting potential, specifically moving toward marriage vows. This happens because they are trying to convince themselves that it's okay to sleep with him.

In the scenario, time passes, and the couple gets to know each other better. Eventually they have sex or make love for the first time and it's good, real good! Now the man is forced to stop and think about the future. In order to do that, he has to pull back and figure some things out. Specifically, he has to decide if he really wants this woman in his life long term. Of course, the woman is way ahead of him. She has already given him everything, so she's all in.

When the woman realizes that he's pulling back she starts to trip. And once she starts tripping, he pulls further away. Then things get really crazy. She is desperately trying to stay close to him while he is desperately trying to get away. The more she holds on, the more she looks like a needy, psycho stalker. The more he pulls away, the more he looks like a trifling, inconsiderate asshole. And, suddenly, it's over.

She gave the man everything. He took it and walked away. He didn't even bother to say "thank you." Listening to this expert taught me a valuable lesson, a lesson I want to pass on to other women... Stop tripping!

~~~~~

A Hopeful Romantic

In the movie *Romancing the Stone,* when Kathleen Turner's editor tell her that she is a hopeless romantic, Turner replies, "Hopeful, I'm a hopeful romantic." That's how I would define myself on most days. In Hollywood movies, romance is all about the fireworks between two people who are lucky enough to collide inside the same orbit. Unfortunately, in real life, we learn that such a collision usually sparks quickly then burns out.

I have a younger cousin who tells me all the time that I send mixed signals out into the universe. I enjoy the emotional, physical, and spiritual connection of a positive male force in my life. So on some days, I may think I'm ready to do whatever it takes to secure a good man and build a great relationship. But on other days, I don't really want to be bothered.

It shouldn't be surprising that the notion of marriage can create monumental angst for strong, independent, career women as well. We are always complaining that it's the man who has a hard time committing, but career women have a hard time with settling down, too. Especially those of us who are looking for something better than the "me-Tarzan-you-Jane" relationship.

Political scientist Elisabeth Noelle-Neumann argues in her Spiral of Silence Theory that people have a hard time publicly expressing their opinion when that opinion is not part of the majority. We all want to belong, to fit in. If our desires are not popular we tend to keep quiet. In other words, it can be difficult to admit out loud what we really want in a man, especially if it does not fit into the norm.

For example, I'm tall for a woman and I feel awkward with a short man. So, someone as tall or taller than me would be appreciated. I'm not sure why I have to feel bad that I'd like to have a taller man. I also want a husband-partner rather than a husband-boss. In other words, I don't want to follow behind a man, even if he's going to the same place I'm going. I want to walk with him side by side. I'm also not looking for a daddy. I had a great father who passed away and nobody can take his place.

I'm looking for a man who will support my success, encourage my dreams, and confirm my values. He has to be a man who can love me in a deep and meaningful way. Someone who appreciates who I am and what I bring to the relationship as an independent, career woman. I want a man secure enough in his own life to let me live mine!

Does it matter if that man is black? Many experts suggest that black women need to open up their marriage searches to men of other races because of the limited availability of black men. And, of course, interracial relationships shouldn't be an issue in the twenty-first century, but for a lot of black women it is still hard to cross over

A lot of black women prefer a black man, that's the reality. As a matter of fact, in the 2014 census data, eighty-six percent of black men who married were married to a black woman and ninety-four percent of married black women were married to a black man. Therefore, the negative messages about limited numbers of available black men and the lack of quality in black male partners are not as prominent as the media suggests. Yet, those are the messages that add to the desperation of single black women, and feed the ego of desirable black men in adverse ways.

For example, some desirable black men don't feel the need to commit because they can pick and choose. When they get bored with one woman they can drop her and move on to the next. All across the country, especially in major cities like Washington, D.C., Atlanta, Baltimore, New Orleans, New York, Chicago, Philadelphia, and Los Angeles the ratio of educated black women to educated black men is too high. I'm not much of a gambler but the odds are not very good.

In my first novel, *So Good: An African American Love Story*, despite some bad choices and dangerous consequences, the protagonist Lisa holds on to her love for black men.

> "She loved black men! She loved the way they walked when they knew a woman was watching. She loved the way they smelled after making love. She loved the way they looked when their muscles contracted on the basketball court, in the weight room or on a construction site. She loved how they spoke with a powerful, comforting rhythm. She loved the soft feel of their smooth brown skin. She loved the rich texture of their course black hair. She loved everything about them."

As a successful African American career woman, I'd like to add a good man into the mix, particularly an African American man. But, as a "hopeful romantic" my focus will be on the man's heart, not his color.

We Are Family

~~~~~

"I sustain myself with the love of family."

Maya Angelou

~~~~~~

A Good Man

My father was a good man. That's what everybody said. He loved us: my mother, my brother, my baby sister, and me. He took good care of us. He made sure we had a good home, food, clothes, and pushed us to get a college education.

This story begins with me coming home from Houston, Texas, where I was living at the time. It was Christmas break and seeing my father busy in front of the stove was not a normal sight. He hummed while he cracked several eggs that sizzled after he dropped them into the hot skillet. He turned strips of bacon over, and then pulled a knife out of the silverware drawer to butter the two slices of toast that had just popped up. My mom, along with daddy's two sisters, sat at the dining room table planning their casino run later that day.

Mom is an artist, a talented, creative soul, yet she has lived seeing the glass as half empty for most of her life. She loved my father and he loved her too. They met in Kansas City when mom was fifteen years old. He was six years older, so she jokes about how she ran for months, but finally gave in and was pregnant by sixteen. They married, and we moved to Des Moines, Iowa where daddy started a janitorial business and purchased a number of rental properties. Life was good, but life was all about daddy.

We lived in the houses daddy wanted us to live in. We bought the cars he wanted to buy. We went on camping and fishing trips, the vacations he wanted. My mother was young and insecure. She grew up in a time when women looked for a man to take care of them. My father did that.

Mom was a housewife for much of her life, which was great for us while growing up. She cooked and cleaned, and raised her three kids. This is most likely where a lot of my hesitancy about marriage and children came from. I always worried that because of my career, I couldn't possibly do as good a job with my own kids as my mother did raising us.

My father worked hard, but he played hard, too. He would leave early in the morning before we got up for school and come home late at night after we were in bed. As I got older, I realized that he was not actually working all of that time. Daddy did a lot of hanging out in the streets with his friends.

Mom told me that she thought about leaving him once when my brother and I were small. This was before my baby sister was born. She said she called her mother to ask for bus money so that we could go back to Kansas City. Mom was surprised when my grandmother asked her:

"What did you do wrong?"

My grandmother asked several other questions: "Do you have food in the refrigerator? Is there a roof over your head? Are the bills paid?" Once mom had answered yes to those questions, my grandmother told her that my father was a good man, and insisted that she stay put.

After that mom made the best of her life, despite the fact that she was depressed through much of it. She slept a lot, because in those days that's what black people did when they were depressed. Therapy or pills was not an accepted or available path.

It was the death of my baby sister that finally forced mom out of her tolerant state. At nineteen-years-old, my sister died of cancer. For mom it meant the glass was now completely empty. In order to survive, she needed to put something back into the glass.

My brother and I were both gone away to college, and daddy was doing his thing, so mom threw herself into school. It was during this time that her talent for art flourished. She earned a bachelor's degree in art from Drake University in Des Moines, Iowa, and even took some graduate courses. Once my mother found the courage to reach for her own dream things started to change.

Sitting in the kitchen that morning as the snow fell, I watched my father carefully organize the plates, silverware, and napkins on the counter. He rinsed the pots and pans arranging them carefully in the dishwasher. Then set large plates of bacon, toast, and eggs in the middle of the counter, and poured glasses of orange juice or milk for everyone.

We dug in, eating, and talking, and laughing. But this was not normal. When I was growing up rarely did my father cook or clean. This miraculous transformation was a key piece of my parents' marriage evolution. An evolution that enabled them to stay married for more than fifty years.

The transformation came years earlier. It was well after midnight when mom opened the door and entered their apartment. The only sound came from the television. She had been in her art studio on campus working on a final project. Daddy was lying on the couch watching reruns of his favorite TV show *Walker Texas Ranger.*

"Where you been all night?" He grunted.

"I had to finish an art project that's due tomorrow," she replied, leaning her portfolio against the hall closet.

"You're spending an awful lot of time up to that school," he barked.

Mom hesitated, and then spit back, "So?"

"You need to clean up that kitchen, it's a mess," he ordered before turning back to his show.

The way mom tells the story is hilarious. She says first she hung up her coat and set her purse on the counter. Then she surveyed the kitchen. The sink held several days worth of dirty dishes. The stove was littered with used pots and pans. The kitchen table was covered with scattered salt and pepper shakers, used napkins, and unopened mail. There were crumbs all over the island counter, next to a half-open loaf of bread. Mom said that all she could do at that moment was walk away. She had not made the mess, and she was too tired to clean it up.

Without saying anything she headed back to the bedroom and slipped into her pajamas. Mom lay in bed for a while and thought about his words. Those thoughts eventually triggered an anger that started to swell until she was suddenly propelled up and forward. An adrenaline surge moved her with determination down the hallway and into the kitchen.

Mom grabbed the large trash can from under the counter and violently thrust each dirty dish from the sink inside, breaking many. Then, she turned on the water and rinsed the empty sink clean. Next, she slid the trashcan to the edge of the dining room table and with a wet dishcloth took a couple of long swipes pushing everything into the trash. Dirty pots and pans were cleared from the stove in the same fashion. Finally, she returned the full trash can to its proper place under the cabinet, turned off the light, and stomped back to the bedroom.

The next morning when mom got up, daddy was gone. But, apparently before he left, he had searched through the trash rescuing the unopened mail, the salt and peppershakers, and a bottle of ketchup. He had also loaded any salvageable dishes, pots and pans, and silverware into the dishwasher and started the wash cycle.

As I ate the delicious breakfast prepared by my daddy that morning, I thought about the major transformation my parents' relationship had survived. By the time daddy died, he had become a really good cook. His favorite meal to cook was fried fish with fried potatoes. He loved to fish so usually the fish was fresh. In his retirement, daddy also became an expert at making Jell-O and baking delicious Betty Crocker cakes.

My father was not perfect, but he was a good man.

~~~~~~

Blue Moon

My cousin Stacey was killed by an abusive husband at the age of twenty-four. He was the man she loved and the man who claimed to love her. Stacey and I were very close growing up, so my thoughts about men and relationships were profoundly shaped by her death.

If there is such a thing as past lives, I must have been abused in one of mine because I have an extreme fear of abuse. I've never been hit or beaten or raped, nothing like that. But, if a man just looks at me the wrong way I'm gone. I don't stick around to find out if he will or won't. It is a fear that I've had for as long as I can remember.

As a matter of fact, I've had dreams about women being abused. Women I don't know. Women from different races. In one dream a man knocks a black woman down a staircase when he hits her with the back of his hand. In another dream a white woman is tied to a bed while a man carves his initials in her chest with a knife. A third dream has an Asian woman and her baby locked in a large animal crate in the basement of a suburban house. I don't see the men clearly in any of my dreams, so my focus is never on the abuser. My focus is always on the pain and terror experienced by these women as the victims of abuse.

Stacey was one of the sweetest people in the world. She was kind and giving. She believed in love. She was determined to love her husband and she needed for him to love her back.

When we were young, we would sit and talk about the future. I was going to college. I wanted to work in television, not in front of the camera, but behind. I thought maybe I'd be a television news producer someday. Stacey always wanted to be married. She wanted love and a family. It was obvious that she would make a great wife because she actually liked taking care of people and she truly wanted to make her man happy.

Our mothers were very close. Stacey and I were carted around daily to garage sales, secondhand shops, and flea markets. We played at each other's houses for hours, sometimes with Barbie dolls (her favorite), and sometimes making up television shows (my favorite). Our families also enjoyed holiday meals, weekend shopping, and summer fishing trips together.

Once Stacey got married I'm not really sure when the beatings started. Truthfully, it probably doesn't matter. What matters is that the beatings didn't stop until she was dead. I was attending the University of Iowa the first time I heard about a late-night trip to the hospital. This beating resulted in a black eye, bloodied nose, and bruised ribs. I called Stacey right away, and she assured me that the family rumors were exaggerated. She would be fine.

It was the third or fourth time when I saw Stacey's wounds for myself and I couldn't help but cry. My mother had called to tell me that Stacey was in the hospital again. After my last class of the day, I drove an hour and a half to Waterloo, Iowa to see her. Stepping inside the hospital room, I had to hide the intense anger that crowded my chest. Her left eye and cheek were blue-black, along with ugly, dark bruises that spread down the right side of her neck and chest. She couldn't move her body without pain. Her left arm was numb where he had stomped her on the floor. Stacey managed a slight smile as I entered the room.

"Hey girl," I said softly, leaning down to kiss the normal side of her face.

"You didn't have to come," she whispered.

At that moment the tears couldn't be stopped. "Of course I had to come," I told her. "I'm not sure what I can do, but I had to come."

She squeezed my hand. "It's okay."

I shook my head. "Stacey, this is not okay."

"He just gets mad and he doesn't think sometimes."

"You mean he gets drunk and doesn't care sometimes," I blurted it out, and then quickly regretted my comment when I saw the devastated look that spread across her face. "Where is he anyway?"

Stacey closed her eyes. "I don't want him to see me like this."

I stared at my cousin in amazement. "What? Stacey, he did this! He needs to see what he did!"

She continued to make excuses for him. "I knew better but I kept pushing him. When he's drinking I know I should leave him alone. He was just in one of his moods."

"Well, you don't have to worry about his moods anymore," I told her. "When you're well enough to leave the hospital, I'll rent a U-Haul to help you pack up and move."

"Move where?" Stacey asked with surprise.

Her question caught me off guard. Of course she was going to leave him. How long would she tolerate this craziness?

"Back to Des Moines with your mother," I replied.

She shook her head. "I'm not moving back."

Stacey spoke so clearly and with such conviction that I was dumbfounded.

"I don't want to be like my mom," she continued. "Going through a bunch of different men and marriages. I'm gonna stay with my husband. I'm gonna make my marriage work."

"You can't be serious, Stacey."

"I'm very serious," she replied. "I love him and if I show him that I plan to stand by his side no matter what, I know things will get better."

I left the hospital a couple of hours later in a fog. I didn't understand her commitment. During the months that followed, I heard about more bruises, more beatings, and more hospital visits. Then, late one night in early June we were attending a family reunion on my mother's side in Oklahoma when Stacey's mother called. Apparently, in one of his drunken rages, Stacey's husband accused her of planning to leave him. The police found her dead body under a bed where she was hiding. He shot her three times with his rifle.

I sat still for a long time after hearing the news. I remember in the background a news reporter excitedly talked about the two full moons that were coming later that month. He explained in great detail how the second full moon is called a "blue moon" because of the specific pattern of lunar phasing and it only happens every two or three years. He quoted from *The Farmer's Almanac* that the term blue moon originated from the word "belewe" in Old English which meant betrayal.

Betrayal was the right word for that moment because Stacey was betrayed by the man she loved. She wanted to keep her marriage together. But, unfortunately for my cousin love brought only abuse, pain, and death. Stacey's death scared me so much that I refused to tolerate extreme attitudes and actions from the men in my life. I never want anyone to love me enough to kill me

Purple Rain

My cousin Darleen was a beautiful girl who made some bad choices. She died before the age of thirty-five. I played with Darleen and Stacey often as a kid. Darleen lived in Kansas City, and her family would visit Des Moines or we would go there regularly. Darleen was very smart. She could have taken her life in any direction, but she chose the streets. She was the complete opposite of Stacey, not the subservient type at all. I've often wondered if her aggressiveness when it came to men was a consequence of the way Stacey's death influenced her.

I've heard a number of stories about Darleen's conflicts with men. After one boyfriend hit her, she waited until he went to sleep, shoved several cans of pork and beans into an empty pillowcase, and commenced to beatin' his ass. She stabbed a man in the leg in the middle of an argument, and shot another guy in the behind as he ran out of the house after a major blow up.

In high school, Darleen fell crazy-in-love and got pregnant. They married, she had the baby, and things were okay for a while. I don't know exactly what happened, but a few years later there was a nasty split. I think this was a turning point for Darleen because she became bitter, moving through life as if she didn't care.

When I heard rumors that Darleen was a prostitute, I didn't believe it. I was in school at the University of Iowa, so I planned a five-hour drive from Iowa City to Kansas City to spend the weekend with her. As soon as I arrived it was like old times. Darleen had an informed opinion about everything, so we laughed and talked for hours. I remember her joking about how fat Fat Albert was. She told me she couldn't watch all of *Roots* because she couldn't stand seeing black people treated like that. She also had plans to buy her daughter a Sunset Malibu Christie doll, the black version of Barbie at the time.

Later that evening, we dropped off her daughter at the baby-sitter's house and headed out to a local club. It was a small, dark, neighborhood joint where Darleen was obviously well known and well respected. Almost everybody made a point to come over to our table and speak. Most of them were men.

As I think back on that night, Darleen watched me as closely as I watched her. If a man she didn't like got too close to me, she stepped in immediately. And when somebody asked me to dance, Darleen answered yes or no for me. One guy who was really drunk flopped down next to me. He was not bad looking, tall with a nice smile. But when he put his arm around my shoulder and licked my neck, Darleen jumped across the table and grabbed him by the throat. She shoved the man off the stool and made him apologize.

An hour or so later, we were joined by two brothers. I immediately noticed a strange link between Darleen and these two men. They were average looking guys. Both had mid-sized afros with walnut brown skin. The older brother was taller with a mustache. He wore black leather pants and a red and black sweater. The younger brother was shorter and heavier. He wore an Adidas-style tracksuit with a gold cross around his neck.

There was nothing really special about either of them, yet I noticed an obvious shift in the power dynamic. It was as if Darleen relinquished her control to them. She got real quiet, and the mood at the table changed.

"My cousin is in college," Darleen told the brothers not long after they both sat down.

"She got brains, huh?" The taller brother nodded, then the chubby one asked, "You gonna be a teacher?"

I didn't have time to respond before they started to tease me. "She gonna be a really pretty school teacher." The younger brother grinned with his gold tooth shining right up front. "Not like the old bats I had to look at."

"She's not going to teach," Darleen corrected him. "She's going to work in television. Someday you might see her on TV doing the news or something."

I had told Darleen earlier that I didn't want to be in front of the camera but when she disapproved I just nodded and smiled.

Throughout the evening several women came bearing gifts for the brothers. They brought drinks, money, and one even handed over what looked like a diamond tennis bracelet.

When the club closed, we headed over to the older brother's house supposedly for an after party. It was a two-story house with a long porch and rickety wooden stairs. The after party was held in his dark basement which resembled a sparsely furnished cave. There was an old, wooden bar and three stools on one side of the room with a couch and coffee table on the other. When we arrived several women were already there.

An hour later, this party consisted of only the two brothers, the four women, Darleen and me. I noticed the tension in the room between Darleen and these women was off the charts. Suddenly, an obvious competition quickly began for the attention of the two guys.

The younger brother was a huge Prince fan, so we listened to a series of songs, like "I Wanna Be Your Lover," "Controversy," and "Dirty Mind." When "Purple Rain" came on, one very aggressive woman, wearing a shiny green dress with matching green eye shadow pulled the younger brother out into the middle of the floor and they started to dance very suggestively. He was soon surrounded by the other women, all of them pulling and rubbing and touching on him.

I glanced over at Darleen who was sitting up under the older brother and watching the show from her seat. Then suddenly, she turned, winked at me, and stood up. Darleen moved gracefully through the red and blue flickering lights into that crowd of women. She took the younger brother's hand and pulled him away. She whispered something in his ear that made them both laugh. Then, she held onto him in a way that told the other girls the competition was over.

On the way back to her apartment, I got up the nerve to ask Darleen about the prostitution rumors, but she never answered me, and I didn't push it. Although we drifted apart over the years, it was Darleen who helped me to understand that the choices we make today lead us into the situations we find ourselves in tomorrow. Darleen chose the streets and with the streets came violence, drugs, and dying much too soon.

~~~~~~

Deal or No Deal

My baby brother's love life is like that game show *Deal or No Deal*. He meets a woman he likes, lets her know that he is not interested in a commitment, but says they can hang out deal or no deal. Some of the women take the deal thinking they can change his mind. Hoping their love will make him commit. After months, sometimes years, they walk away hurt and disillusioned because just like he said up front, he didn't commit.

Only two years younger than I am, my brother has never been married either. He's a nice looking man, successful, a great guy, and very respectful to women. He loves women, all women: short, tall, skinny, thick, light skinned, dark skinned, smart, simple, and everything in-between. Many of the women he's dated would take him back in a heartbeat because he makes them feel special. When he's with them, they may not be the one, but he makes them feel like they could be.

I once asked my brother if he ever thought he would find the right woman and marry her. We were both in our early thirties, sitting in an Ethiopian restaurant in Washington, D.C. where he lived and worked at the time. I tore off a piece of the spongy bread and scooped up a clump of spicy greens just before I spoke.

"So, do you think you'll ever find somebody you want to spend the rest of your life with?" I asked.

He shrugged. "I don't know."

"Do you want to find somebody to spend the rest of your life with?" I added.

He shrugged again. "I guess."

"I don't understand the problem. As an educated, black woman I have limited choices, but as an educated black man there are endless possibilities all around you."

He took a moment to think about it, while I shoved more greens and sponge bread into my mouth.

"The problem is," he finally answered, "I can be with an amazing, intelligent, gorgeous woman. She has everything I want. But then, another smart, exceptional, beautiful woman walks by, and I wonder what would it be like to be with her."

I had to close my mouth because it was hanging open in shock.

"So you can't settle down with somebody you know is a good woman because there are other potentially good women out there?"

"I figure when I'm with the person I'm supposed to settle down with she will be enough, and I will stop wanting other women."

"Are you serious?"

"Maybe another way to say it is that I haven't met the woman I can't say goodbye to."

I love my baby brother, but now I knew he was looney-tunes.

"You have to stop yourself!" I fussed at him. "It's about being an adult. Taking control of your life and not acting on those whims. There will always be other women who pique your interest. You have to make the choice to walk away from that temptation."

He was only half listening.

"You asked and I told you. That's how I feel," he insisted. "The woman who inspires me to walk away from temptation is the woman that I will probably end up with."

I stopped arguing. Somehow he had made it the woman's fault that his moral and spiritual compass was warped. And as long as he didn't take responsibility for his actions he could shake off the devastation that his commitmentphobia caused those women who took the deal hoping for something more.

"You know there is a positive to never getting married," he added.

"What's that?"

"I never have to experience divorce!"

For my brother his honesty is a shield of righteousness. If the woman doesn't want what he's offering she should walk away. I guess he has a point. It's not his fault that women ignore what he says thinking they can change him. We need to listen to what men tell us. We need to pay attention and believe.

My brother often brings his women home to meet the family. No matter how hard I try, I can't get him to understand that bringing a woman home says something special to her about their relationship. It doesn't mean the same thing for him.

It's frustrating to talk to these women because I know what they are going through. I have to create a phony smile knowing they'll be gone in a few months or maybe a year or two. It's hard because I've been there too. I think he's the man of my dreams, but instead, just like them, my heart gets stepped on. Maybe when I feel sorry for them, I'm actually feeling sorry for myself.

My mother jokes that he will settle down someday when he's old and tired and needs somebody to take care of him. When that time comes, I'm sure there will be plenty of women willing to step into the role. But for now, my baby brother follows the same mantra as Auntie Mame, "Life is a banquet and most poor suckers are starving to death."

~~~~~~

Hoochies, Hotties & Hoes

Sex is everywhere. It is used to sell everything from clothes and cars to soft drinks and toothpaste. I worry about my daughter in today's society. She and other young girls in her generation are having a hard time loving themselves. They don't celebrate their own beauty, and they don't understand how precious their bodies are.

Well-known models and celebrities now sport the skimpy, erotic clothing that, at one time, was worn only by prostitutes and strippers. Because of women's liberation some argue that it is okay for women to dress any way they want. But, I have to agree with Chris Rock "If you put on a police uniform people will think you're a policeman."

My daughter attended a Christian school from kindergarten to eighth grade. It wasn't the original plan, but once she got there it seemed like a good place for her to be. We attended church regularly as she was growing up because I thought that raising her up with the Lord would give her a good foundation. But, by high school she became a typical teenager with a funky attitude and a messy room.

I worry about my daughter's future in this sex-driven, pop-culture world. It is definitely a world where love and sex are presented as if they mean the same thing. It is a world where young men have little respect for young women and young women don't know how to demand respect for themselves.

I know I can't blame it all on the media, but the abundance of negative stereotypes and labels tied to black men and women in movies, TV shows, and rap music is frightening. The bad boy or thug has been glamorized and normalized in the media causing young, impressionable girls to feel it is okay to accept less.

I served as the keynote speaker for an awards ceremony in a major city a few years ago. After the event, some of the older folks decided to join some of the younger folks at the local night spot. As older people normally do, we got there early and found good seats because most of the younger crowd didn't arrive until well after midnight.

As I sat and watched the interactions among that young crowd, I was dumbfounded. The sexual exploitation of women in that club was off the chain, as the kids used to say. Men were humping women and women were humping poles. It was like a live music video from *BET Uncut*. Men touched and rubbed and grabbed wherever they wanted, and women encouraged their erotic attention.

One woman on the dance floor reached for a guy who was passing by. I don't know if they knew each other or not, but after she grabbed him, she immediately turned her back, bent over, and began pumping her behind up into his crotch. He held onto her hips with both hands, and they went at it doggy style. OMG! All I could think was that this is the world my daughter has to learn to navigate.

When my child was about ten years old we were watching a Disney television show and I asked her if she thought the boy on television was cute. She turned up her nose and complained. "Mom that's gross." I hid my smile because that was the response I wanted to hear.

Now, a graduate from public high school, her last four years were not as sheltered as the first eight, so it's not so gross anymore. My baby's grown up, and I'm trying to help her love herself enough to demand respect. I always say if movies, television programs, and videos show kids five, seven, and nine years old liking each other and kissing, why is it surprising that many kids are sexually active by ten, twelve, and fourteen?

Kids today are not allowed to enjoy just being kids and that bothers me. They are constantly pushed into adult situations. On a vacation in Florida, I was sitting on the beach with a mango margarita in one hand and a good book in the other when I noticed a five-year-old child waddling across the sand in a bikini. We all know what a bikini is designed to suggest.

Women wear bikinis so that men can admire their bodies. When men see a girl in a bikini they think about sex. So, why would a parent put their five-year-old in a bikini? Why would the clothing industry make a bikini for a five year old? At eighteen, twenty-five, or thirty-years-old it may be appropriate, but a five-year-old child in a bikini sends the wrong message.

I have a number of pet peeves. Another one with the clothing industry involves those pants with words written across the butt. My daughter came home from a visit with her father wearing a pair of sweatpants with "princess" or "sassy" or "juicy" or something scrawled across her backside. She was maybe nine or ten years old, and I exploded. What is the purpose for placing words on the back of pants across a woman's behind? It is to encourage men look at her behind. I don't want a man looking at my nine or ten-year-old daughter's behind.

In my classes, I teach about capitalism's exploitation of consumers in our society. The clothing industry is pushing a trend called "tweening." Sociologist Juliet Schor calls it "age compression." It is the practice of targeting products and marketing messages originally designed for older teens and adults to younger kids.

In the summer of 2005, the popular culture gurus decided to release a new movie based on a 1980's television show called *Dukes of Hazzard*. Blue jean shorts called Daisy Dukes were popularized in the original television series and again from the movie. I went to several different stores that summer trying to find a decent pair of shorts for my child. Everything she tried on was cut like Daisy Dukes. They were so short that the cheeks of her behind hung out. We finally had to go into the boy's department to purchase a couple of pairs of shorts for her to wear that summer.

The media stays on my pet peeve list. Media images have black girls all mixed up when it comes to beauty. My daughter grew up thinking that she is fat and ugly. But she is definitely not fat or ugly. She's a beautiful black girl with a curvy frame. She is not rail thin like some of her white friends. However, being raised in a predominantly white environment has locked her into the traditional media hype and warped her vision of beauty. According to the media, beauty is having blonde hair, blue eyes, and wearing a size zero.

Every time I get the chance to offer an alternative view I do, despite the fact that she tells me she hates being preached at. I keep trying anyway because every now and then I see a flash of understanding that lets me know something I said or did might be sinking in. I've shown her photos from *Essence* magazine of beautiful, black women with natural hair. I've bribed her to watch the *Black Girls Rock Awards* show on BET with me. I've even pointed out the beauty of her equally curvy Latina friend.

I know that selfies on social media are sometimes questionable. And as a parent I worry that this social media craze is going too far. But as my baby gets older and more mature, I have faith that putting on makeup and slipping the neckline of her top off of her shoulder in a sexy pose for Facebook or snap chat means she is not only recognizing, but documenting her beauty. It shows me that my child is learning to love and appreciate her body, and there is nothing wrong with that.

~~~~~~

Late Bloomers

Older women are like late blooming perennials in fall gardens offering bold colors and rich textures. Their beauty like the deep purple asters, bright gold sunflowers, rust-colored day lilies, and scarlet hibiscus plants makes me happy. Several of my aunties were late bloomers. They are women who have muddled through years of bad relationships, until they finally found the love they were looking for.

For example, in her late thirties, my Aunt Ellen lived in California and worked as a computer analyst at a large bank. She was short, shapely, and cocoa-brown skinned with lots of sass. In her younger life she had several terrible boyfriends. I remember one from the 1970's that my brother and I called green slime. After they took us to see a monster movie called *The Green Slime*, a few weeks later he showed up in an ugly, bright green leisure suit. I also remember overhearing a few conversations between my aunt and my mother confirming that designation.

Aunt Ellen's love story began many years later with a two-hour commute in horrific Los Angeles freeway traffic. After a long day at work she would return home, eat dinner, relax, go to bed, wake up, and start all over again. One morning she was rushing to work, and a traffic policeman stationed at an intersection held up his hand for her to stop. When he finally waved her forward, she pushed the gas pedal down and cut her eyes at him as she passed.

Soon this was happening quite often. Other cars would jet right through the intersection, but as soon as she got close this same policeman would lift up his hand for her to stop. Aunt Ellen didn't know it at the time, but this traffic officer was working with a buddy who sat up on the hill and watched for her car, a 1974 green, Ford Torino. When the officer up on the hill saw her coming he would give his buddy a call.

This went on for several months. The policeman would lift his hand to stop her, and she would get pissed. Finally, one day after he waved her through, Aunt Ellen glanced back to see the big smile on his face. Over the next few weeks, she dressed a little sexier, and made sure her makeup was perfect whenever she rolled through that intersection.

Then one morning, Aunt Ellen decided to take a chance. Before leaving her house she wrote her name and phone number on a piece of paper, then slipped it in her jacket pocket. The drive to work seemed to take forever. The traffic was worse than normal, but it was worth it when she saw him standing at his usual corner. He raised his hand to stop her and she obeyed. But this time, just before he waved her through she reached in her pocket, pulled out the piece of paper, and thrust it into his hand. Within a year they were married, and their marriage lasted for almost twenty years until her death.

My Aunt Lora was in her early forties when she met Mr. Right at a popular juke joint in Kansas City. Aunt Lora liked to gamble, so she spent a lot of time at the dog and horse races, casinos, and riverboats. She was cornbread-colored, slim and very pretty. Her love life consisted of a bunch of sorry characters early on, until this one made love real.

They bumped into each other at various gambling spots over a number of years. She thought he was cute, but he was married. Eventually, she married too. But later circumstances changed. They ran into each other when he was separated from his wife and she was single.

For their first official date they went to the movies to see Spike Lee's *She's Gotta Have It*. It was 1986, and they had heard a lot about the film student from New York University who was launching his career based on the story of sex-crazed Nola Darling, and the three men she loved.

A few months later they moved in together. When I asked Aunt Lora how he proposed. She explained:

"One night we were talking about a mutual friend who was getting married. He looked me straight in the face and said 'I'm going to marry you.'" They set a date that night, but they had been drinking, and the next morning he didn't remember the conversation.

Once she reminded him of the conversation, he stayed true to his word. A couple of months later they were married in the Kansas City courthouse. Their marriage has lasted for more than 30 years.

My Aunt Benita said she was surprised when she ended up with a man she's known all her life. She remembered him as a bully when they were kids, at least he ran with a group of bullies. In one story, his friends were teasing a girl, and they took what they thought was her purse. Instead it was Aunt Benita's purse. When he found out about the mistake he made sure she got her purse back.

It was 2001 when they reconnected at a forty-year high school reunion. Aunt Benita said she didn't pay much attention to him until her sister told her he was flirting. They kept in touch, and a few months later he got up the nerve to tell Aunt Benita that he had loved her all of his life, but he was afraid of her. She told him she didn't like him at all in high school because he thought he was hot stuff.

At first, when he talked about coming back into her life Aunt Benita said she really wasn't interested. She had been married before, and she was done taking care of other people. She didn't want to worry about what somebody else was going to eat or if their clothes got washed. But his persistence eventually won her over.

Once they had spent some time together, she described him as a really nice guy who would give you his last. Aunt Benita and her beau made a long distance relationship work for more than fifteen years. They traveled back and forth between Iowa and Arkansas. He bought an engagement ring that she wore sometimes, but they never married.

Admitting that she's sometimes selfish and moody, Aunt Benita appreciated the fact that this man understood and gave her the space she needed. Reading the *Bible*, doing yard work, and cooking together became a normal part of their routine when he was in town. At one point, she even joked that he might be too good for her.

My Aunt Benita loved working in her yard. She used to say "There are some flowers that bloom later than others, but whenever or however they bloom they are all beautiful."

I like to remember these stories about my aunties who were late bloomers. As I get older they help me feel confident that it is never too late.

Kindred Spirits

~~~~~

"Lots of people want to ride with you in the limo. What you want is someone who will take the bus with you when the limo breaks down."

Oprah Winfrey

~~~~~~

Good Dick

When the phone rings I look at the caller ID and grin because it's Alyssa, one of my very best friends.

"Girl, what happened to all the good dick?" Alyssa started lamenting before I could get the phone up to my ear.

"What?"

"It used to be everywhere. If one man wasn't acting right you kicked him to the curb, stood out on your front porch, and pointed into the crowd, "Next!""

"Alyssa, girl, you're crazy."

"I'm serious. I need love in my life, but these men out here in L. A. are pathetic."

I take a moment to think about the last three men Alyssa told me about and chuckle. There was the Muslim artist who sold incense on the side of the road; the possibly, down-low security guard who still lived with his mother; and the lookin'-for-a-home, just released from jail embezzler.

"Maybe I need to reconsider Mr. Sun's offer," Alyssa mumbled as an afterthought.

"Who's Mr. Sun?" This was a new one. I didn't have any background on him.

"He's my sixty-year-old gardener. He asked me out for lunch the other day."

"See there are interested men around." My encouragement

falls on deaf ears.

"He's old, Venise, and he only comes up as high as my belly button."

We laugh hard since we are both tall women and prefer taller men.

"Now see, that's the problem with successful black women like you," I tease. "You're too damn picky."

"I just want one good black man. Is that too much to ask?"

"Apparently. Maybe you should look outside of the race."

"I can't help it if I have a preference for strong, intelligent, black men."

"At least you have options. I'm in Iowa and ain't nothing happening here, black, white or in-between."

"I don't understand why you stay in Iowa."

I take a deep breath. "It probably sounds crazy, but I think I'm here because there's nothing happening, less drama, and more control. I'm getting too old to deal with the disappointment of a bad relationship. It takes me a lot more time to recover now than it used to."

"See, that's the problem with mature, career-oriented black women like you," Alyssa jokes. "You want to control everything."

We laugh some more.

Alyssa's other line clicks. "Uh oh girl it's Marcus, that real estate agent I met on the Internet. I got to go."

"Wait a minute. He's the one who disappears for months at a time, right?" I ask in disbelief.

"Yep. I guess he's back."

"You'd probably do better calling Mr. Sun."

"Please girl, shoot me if I get that desperate. Bye."

~~~~~~

What's Love Got to Do With It?

The notion of a woman looking for a rich man to take care of her is not new. According to Nickolaus Hines, the term "gold digger" was used in a 1915 novel by Virginia Brooks called *My Battle with Vice*. In the story a woman attaches herself to several men for their money. On October 13, 1919, a play actually titled *The Gold Diggers* opened at the Lyceum Theater in New York. And in 1923, a movie with the same name was released followed by a second movie *The Gold Diggers of Broadway* in 1929.

In the lyrics of his 2005 hit song "Gold Digger," Kanye West warned men to be careful of women who were after their money. He sang, "She got one of yo' kids, got you for eighteen years." So, when it was announced that Kim Kardashian was pregnant with his first child the Internet lit up with jokes about Kanye ignoring his own warning. However, the couple is hanging in there. They are married with three children.

Kim Kardashian was considered a gold digger because according to various media sources her claim to fame was a 2007 sex tape with actor and singer Ray J, and a seventy-two day marriage to NBA star Kris Humphries.

One of my favorite reality shows *Millionaire Matchmaker* is clearly tied to the idea of gold digging. Wouldn't that be wonderful? All you need to do is join the Millionaire's Club and Patti Stanger will hook you up!

Sometimes I don't agree with Patti's advice. She seems somewhat old-fashioned when it comes to dating. Women can have a little independence, but the man is always king. Patti coaches the men to romance their dates in order to make them feel special. She pushes the fairy tale and encourages her club members to buy into that fantasy. Her club has two main rules. First, she instructs all clients that they are not to engage in sex before monogamy. Second, she limits their alcohol intake to two glasses on dates because she believes more can cloud their judgment.

Usually, the millionaires are men, but every now and then she brings on a woman. Probably the most pathetic episode I've seen involved a desperate, plus-sized, female millionaire. The woman was attracted to the typical young, hot guys. So, Patti tried to be honest and explain that many of the guys who are serious about fitness would not be attracted to anybody who wasn't. She encouraged the millionairess to choose appropriately.

The lady didn't want to hear it. She chose a young, hot guy for her date anyway. The evening was really sad to watch. They had a romantic dinner on a boat and she basically offered to pay the hot guy to be with her. When he mentioned wanting to start a business, she said she could make it happen. She told him that he would look good in a Maserati and that she would love to take him out shopping. What's love got to do with it?

I understand that reality shows are not actually reality because much of the content is staged, but the problem is that a lot of viewers buy into those images. After shooting for months, producers and editors pull out the most interesting and exciting segments hoping to create a good show. Too often those interesting and exciting segments support problematic stereotypes like gold digging.

One VH1 series that literally made my skin crawl was *Flavor of Love*. Watching that show each week was like watching a disaster, I wanted to turn away but just couldn't. The show featured an old school, hip hop artist from Public Enemy known as Flavor Flav. The fact that Flavor Flav was able to find three seasons worth of women willing to degrade themselves on television is evidence that many women in our society today are desperate.

Flavor Flav didn't even bother to learn their names. Instead he gave them offensive labels like Buckwild, Krazy, Hottie, and Deelishis. He called a set of twins Thing One and Thing Two. In a 2014 article on the *Vulture* website, one of the producers described the women on the show as mirroring the Stockholm Syndrome because they got caught up in the experience too quickly. A reporter for *Jezebel* called the show sad yet fascinating.

The women on the show schemed and cried and fought for the so-called love of this sorry character. With his top hat, bright colored suits, shiny shoes, gold teeth, and the big clock hung around his neck, Flavor Flav looked just like a zip coon buffoon stereotype. It was obvious that love had nothing to do with it.

On New Years Eve in 2012, Hugh Hefner married for the third time at eighty-six-years-old. His bride was twenty-six. And I remember a big story about the twenty-four-year-old stripper and model Anna Nicole Smith who married eighty-nine-year-old J. Howard Marshall. He died two years later, and Smith won a significant amount of money in the court battle.

Today, gold diggers are so prominent that a rookie NBA transition program has been designed to help new, financially successful pro-athletes maneuver in certain areas like keeping track of their money, building their image/brand, and staying away from a certain kind of women.

Gold digging is not just a problem for men. In the media you can find plenty of stories about rich women who are also dealing with this problem. Halle Berry was ordered to pay her baby daddy Gabriel Aubrey sixteen thousand dollars a month for child support when they broke up. Surprisingly, Roseanne Barr did not insist on a prenup when she married Tom Arnold in 1990 and that four year marriage cost Roseanne fifty million dollars.

I had an interesting conversation about gold digging with a good friend. He's a fifty-something psychologist who has never been married. When I asked him why he had not found someone to settle down with his answer surprised me. He said he was looking for a relationship that was truly about love. He wants a woman to love him for him not because he can fill a slot she has created.

He went on to explain that a lot of the women he meets are older, and they have decided they are ready to marry, so they are looking for a man to fill a slot.

To be honest, I'm not sure my friend will ever find that woman or that kind of love at this stage in his life because that kind of love happens when we're not worried about the future. That is our mental state when we're young, and life is still wide open with possibilities. As women get older, establish their own careers, and start to understand how important financial stability is they don't have to create a slot, it erupts like a sinkhole.

A career woman usually looks for a man who is her equal. He should be someone who is financially secure. Of course, we recognize that a good man may not have the kind of money we have, but equal does not have to be about money. When I go on a date to a restaurant or movie I don't expect him to pay every time. I can pay for both of us or go dutch sometimes. I also don't mind sharing. If he is having a hard time financially, I might offer him a loan, but I expect to be paid back even if we break up.

In today's capitalistic society we are told to focus on ourselves and get all we can. Many of the movies we see and the books we read suggest that it is okay to be selfish. Jen Kim in a 2011 article from *Psychology Today* reports that a school in China teaches women to be the best gold diggers they can be. The women are taught to be respectful, caring and subservient, so that wealthy men will pay up to five thousand dollars to meet the perfect bachelorettes.

Sometimes, you have to ask the question "What's love got to do with it?"

~~~~~~

Age Versus Beauty

"Girl, I remember when I used to be sexy," Alyssa whined on the opposite end of the phone.

"You know you still look good," I assured her like a true friend.

"I've got to get some weight off my big ass," she continued not listening to me.

"You know it is not about weight."

"I know, I know. Too many of those cute girls in my office, those twenty somethings with the long hair and tiny waistlines are complaining. Apparently everybody's in trouble."

I nod my head even though she can't see me because we're on the phone. "And you know your age is not the issue either, right? My students are constantly crying the blues about the lack of available men and they are young and sexy."

"I can't shake this age thing. It feels like a vampire is sucking the life out of me!"

I shake my head. Alyssa is one of the funniest people I know.

"Why do you think I got my bad knees replaced? I was fifty-something feeling like a ninety-year old. Even though it was temporary, I was embarrassed every time I had to use the walker."

"I don't know why you were embarrassed," she joked. "When I got my hip replaced last year I was all up in the Cheese cake Factory with my walker. I even flirted with my cute little Hispanic waiter."

I could see it in my mind. Alyssa in her high heels and tight dress hobbling over to the table on her walker and winking at the waiter after she sat down. I had to laugh.

"So what you got going on for the weekend?" Alyssa asked.

I shook my head. "Nothing. I'm tired. I'm looking forward to spending my Friday night at home, in my bed, in front of the television."

"You know it's not good for us to get too comfortable at home by ourselves."

"I know. It would be nice to have somebody laying next to me, but he would have to knock on my front door."

"That's not going to happen. You gotta get out there and look. Maybe I'll go out tonight."

"Good for you. Go out there and make me proud."

"You can't give up."

"I haven't given up. I'm just avoiding that vicious cycle: look for him, find him, meet him, date him, care about him, love him, lose him, then start all over again."

"Maybe you should try an older man. There's almost a twenty-year difference between me and the guy I'm seeing."

"I don't have a problem with an older man, as long as he's a good man."

"Mine is a sweetie. He sent flowers, chocolates, and a stuffed panda bear for my birthday."

"That's what I'm talking about a man who remembers your birthday. So why are you complaining?"

Alyssa hesitated. "It's just not the same..."

"What's not the same?"

"I know this sounds trifling."

"What?"

She paused, "The sex."

"Have him take Viagra or Cialis or something."

She grunts. "He's seventy Venise. I don't want to kill him."

"Well, do you want love or sex?"

"Both?"

I chuckle. "What a greedy black woman you are."

"I'm not trying to be greedy, but I have needs."

I swallow hard. "You know what I would worry about with an older man?"

"What?"

"Holding onto him."

"Girl please. Why would you worry about that?"

"I don't know. It's one thing to break up with a younger man. Just the fact that you had him for a while makes you feel good, but if you can't hold onto an old man that could be devastating."

"Well, I'm not worried. One thing I've learned since we got together is that a sixty or seventy-year-old sees my fifty-year-old behind as sexy."

Alyssa laughs deeply, and I follow her lead.

"He can act a fool if he wants to," Alyssa continues. "He done opened my eyes to a whole new pool of eligible men."

I imagined her with her hand on her titanium hip as she spoke.

"A younger man makes you feel young too."

"Yeah, but how long can you keep up with him?"

"I could sure have a lot of fun trying."

There's a lull in the conversation as we both think about age versus beauty.

"Hey, if you want to be a cougar go for it," Alyssa finally blurts out.

"I dated this younger guy years ago. He was very mature for his age. Served in the Army Reserves and looked good in that uniform. Umm, umm, umm, brother was fine. He had deep, smooth, ebony skin, a sweet personality, and he was a fabulous lover."

"So what happened?"

"I didn't see him as a keeper. I thought I needed somebody older, more advanced in their career, more secure."

"Your loss was somebody else's gain."

"Yep," I reply taking a moment to reminisce.

"This conversation is depressing. We keep talking about taking a cruise. Let's really do it next year," Alyssa suggests.

"I actually found a couple of interesting black singles cruises on the Internet. One is called 'Grown and Sexy' and the other is 'Blacks Over 40.'"

"Send me the info. You know I keep my bags packed."

~~~~~~

From Fact to Fiction

Writing my second novel *All of Me: A Voluptuous Tale* was more difficult than I imagined. It was not my autobiography, but a number of the experiences I wrote about were true. The main character Serpentine struggled with her self-esteem, and her self-esteem was closely tied to her weight. The story explored how Serpentine's weight had yo-yoed up and down all of her life, and she basically needed to learn how to love herself just the way she was.

I started the book with Serpentine's character in the hospital after a failed suicide attempt. In the many interviews and book signings I did to promote the novel, I feel bad that I never answered that one question truthfully. Talk show hosts, journalists, and book club fans asked if I had ever thought about or attempted suicide. The question made me cringe. I was ashamed to answer it truthfully. Weak, crazy, even stupid people consider suicide. So my answer was always no. But that wasn't true. At one point in my life, I did think seriously about leaving this earth. In fact, I even planned my exit.

I didn't want it to be painful, so cutting my wrists or shooting myself or jumping off a tall building or swallowing a bunch of pills was out. I decided the easiest way to die would be with carbon monoxide poisoning. I could start up the car in the garage late one night and just go to sleep. It would be a calm, peaceful way to go.

I never followed through in real life, but in *All of Me* when

Serpentine grows tired of her struggle my research and planning came in handy. Unlike me, Serpentine doesn't spend a lot of time thinking about it. She just writes a quick note, enters her garage, starts the car, and slips under a warm, cotton blanket to wait.

Serpentine's character is a lot like me. She doesn't fully appreciate the blessings in her life. She blames everything that goes wrong on her weight. She looks in the mirror and doesn't see her own beauty. She doesn't understand that beauty is so much more than what is on the outside.

There are so many misconceptions when it comes to size in America. The Textile Institute launched a study in 2016 that found the average woman wears a size twelve to sixteen. So, the media's focus on super models and celebrities who range from size zero to three is ridiculous. Some fashion designers have started something called "vanity sizing" where a size twelve is labeled smaller. For example, the label says a size nine, but it is cut large enough to fit a size twelve.

But, that's not the answer because size is not the problem. The problem is that stereotypes of women's bodies are so prominent that the average woman sees herself as inadequate. Women on television, in movies, music videos, and advertising are constructed as images of perfection. A perfect woman, a beautiful woman, is young and thin which means the rest of us are seen as inferior.

Many of us are making ourselves sick trying to attain this stereotypical perfection. Eating disorders like bulimia and anorexia are prominent among younger women, including African American women.

Crazy diets are adopted like the "Cigarette Diet" where you smoke a cigarette rather than eat when you're hungry replacing the fat with lung cancer. The "Chewing Diet" suggests that you chew your food intensively then spit it out rather than swallow it. Some diets want you to eat unlimited amounts of one thing like cabbage soup or grapefruits. If I have to eat only cabbage soup or grapefruit all day you might as well put me in the ground right now. Plus, there are other crazy things women do in an effort to fit into that unrealistic norm like daily laxatives, starvation, tape-worms, and surgery.

As I travel around the country, I am amazed to see how many men love big women. Visiting Atlanta recently, I noticed that there are more big women with men than skinny ones. And they don't seem to mind holding hands with or kissing their plus-sized beauties in public. At a fundraising event in Washington, D.C., I watched a man knock over a little woman trying to get next to a bigger one. Also, whenever I go to a restaurant or the mall in Chicago, there are just as many plus-sized women with men on their arms as smaller women.

Unfortunately, my lifelong obsession with my weight has always been a problem. When I was growing up this really skinny model Twiggy was popular. I was a size ten or twelve and looked pretty good, but I thought I was too heavy. In *All of Me*, Serpentine talks about how looking at her pictures from high school makes her mad because she looked good and couldn't enjoy it. That part was real.

I had to make some changes in my attitude in order to change my situation. As a matter of fact, I wrote *All of Me* because I wanted plus-sized women to think about themselves differently. We need to be more confident. We need to love ourselves just the way we are.

I sometimes watch the reality show *RuPaul's Drag Race*. In the show, a group of cross-dressing men compete in various challenges to be named America's next drag superstar. It is amazing how some look like really beautiful women. At the end of each episode RuPaul says

"Honey, if you can't love yourself, how the hell you gonna love somebody else?"

To that, I always reply, Amen!

~~~~~~

Janet Jackson - Control

Many college kids in the seventies tried drugs. Back then drugs were rampant on campuses across the country. To be honest, I tried a few myself: marijuana, cocaine, and even heroin once. I was lucky, I didn't like the way drugs made me feel. I didn't like being out of control. The mind goes fuzzy, the senses are weakened, and your body may not function the way you want or need.

In those days people could experiment with drugs because they were more natural. Most were plants grown in dirt just like carrots, potatoes, and corn. Today, drugs are rarely sold in their natural state. They are cut with synthetic chemicals making it almost impossible to get them out of your system. And of course, this is not an accident. Dealers want to get you hooked because if you can't kick the habit it is better for business. There are many articles on the Internet that talk about how drugs sold on the street are often laced with bug spray, gasoline, hair spray, Epsom Salt, silicon, and other junk.

Taking control was not something that came automatically for me. I first realized the importance of control in high school at a party one Saturday night. This guy I had a crush on sauntered into the room, and my heart raced. He was a cutie pie, so I just knew we would be awesome together. I'm sitting at a table with my girls trying to get his attention, but not too obviously. I stared. I smiled. I even went to get something to drink, and I accidentally brushed up against him on purpose.

Before any of my subtle tactics could work one of the more experienced girls in our high school stepped to him. She whispered something in his ear, and they strolled out of the door together. A week later she was calling herself his girlfriend. That's when I decided if I was going to get what I wanted I had to take control.

Over the years, what I've found is that taking control in some ways means fewer problems, and that can make life a lot easier. I'm not saying things never go wrong. But there is a difference when the problem is something that could have been avoided compared to something that comes out of nowhere.

To some, my need for control is not always seen as a positive characteristic, especially in relationships. One night, I was headed to a concert with a date. I asked him a very simple question: "Do you have the tickets?" Now for me this is a normal question. I always stop and make sure I have everything. For instance, before I leave to go to a meeting, I make sure I have all the necessary paperwork. Before I leave for the airport, I make sure I have my itinerary and ID. Before I leave for a class, I make sure I have any assignments or books I might need.

When I asked him that question he scowled at me. "What? Do you think I'm too stupid to remember the tickets?"

Some men see it as control if you ask them to take out the garbage or help cook a meal or try a different sexual position that works better for you. The way I look at it, I should not have to ask my man to take out the garbage. If the garbage can is overflowing and needs to be emptied he can see it's a problem just as I can. As a matter of fact, I don't want to ask him to take out the trash. I want him to care enough to just do it.

In a lot of relationships money equals control. Because money is the leading cause of many arguments, fights, and break ups between couples, you would think that a successful, independent black woman who can take care of herself financially would be a good partner. Unfortunately, that control issue sometimes gets in the way. When a woman has her own money some men feel like their control is taken away or limited. And maybe they're right. Most women who have financial stability are not going to take on a subservient or dependent role. They are less likely to accept abuse or cheating or disrespect. Basically, they don't have to put up with a lot of bullshit.

Yet, being a career-minded, independent woman doesn't mean that we love a man any less or that we can't respect the love that he offers. I've worked hard to distinguish myself and establish my career. When I meet a potential mate who expects me to apologize for my success or ignores the value of my accomplishments, it's not a good match.

I have a cousin who complains about Tyler Perry movies. She doesn't like his depictions of successful, black women. She says too many of them are uppity, controlling, and condescending. Examples include the characters played by Janet Jackson and Tasha Smith in *Why Did I Get Married* or Gabrielle Union in *Daddy's Little Girls*.

My cousin argues that Perry's primary message in these movies seems to be that successful women should lower their standards because they are too high for a lot of men to live up to. She believes that Tyler Perry should push a different message. He should tell those men to step up their game and do what they need to do to reach our higher standards.

Some women, especially as they get older have tried lowering their standards. They might spice up their needy side or camouflage their achievements trying to be what the man wants. But, it doesn't last long because the soul can't thrive inside a lie.

It took a while for me to figure out that it's my responsibility to create the kind of relationship I want. I can't expect anyone else to do it for me, and it is not going to magically happen. The best way to build a good relationship is to figure out what makes me happy and move toward it. If I'm not happy, then he probably won't be happy either.

As a successful, independent, career woman I don't need a man to take care of me. That means I can, literally, afford to marry for love. The right man will appreciate the financial freedom that comes from two successful careers. And, we can enjoy the kind of love that's possible without the struggle for money.

~~~~~~

Animal Crackers

I loved animal crackers as a child. My favorite animals were elephants and camels because they were unique. I would eat all of the others first: the horse, donkey, cat, dog, lion, cow, goat, bear, tiger, hippopotamus, and rhinoceros. Then I would savor my two favorites at the end.

I remember sitting the colorful, circus-themed, red, yellow and blue box in front of me on top of the dining room table to study it. At the top of the box was the name *Barnum's Animal Crackers*. The box was divided into four squares with cages filling each square. Different boxes had different animals in the cages. One box might show a polar bear, lion, gorilla, and elephant. Another box would replace the lion and gorilla with a monkey and tiger.

I love animals. Tears come to my eyes when I see one of those promotions on television about animal rescue organizations. They show images of the mistreated dog with one eye swollen shut, and the shivering cat that's missing a big patch of fur, and a horse with a bandaged leg that can barely walk. I don't understand how anyone can be so cruel as to hurt an innocent animal.

My mom always told me to pay close attention to how a guy treats animals. She explained that, "People who hurt animals are usually cruel people and they are also more likely to hurt you."

We were sitting at the kitchen table. I was maybe fourteen or fifteen. She continued: "A man who is cruel to animals lacks compassion, and he can be a mean person."

"I can't stand those people who keep their dogs outside chained up in the backyard, especially during the winter." I said.

"That's not quite what I mean," mom replied through a smile. "As long as he feeds the dog and cares for the dog properly, gives him a dog house with a blanket to lay on for warmth, it's okay."

I frowned. "Yeah, but winters in Iowa are too cold for any animal to live outside. I think it's mean."

"What about the animals that live outside naturally in the winter?" Mom asked. "Squirrels, rabbits, deer, and foxes are created to live outside."

I looked over at our spoiled mutt who was stretched out in the middle of the living room floor. He definitely wouldn't make it if he had to stay outside in the winter.

"But, what's the purpose of having a dog if you leave him chained up outside? If something happens in the house, like somebody breaks in, he can't even protect you."

Mom was amused by how determined I was to make my case.

"Not everybody keeps a dog in the house like we do," she shrugged. "People care for their animals differently."

I refused to accept it. I have always had a dog in my life. I have loved every one of my dogs, and they have loved me back, unconditionally. When I walk into the house my dog is sincerely happy to see me. He whines for me to acknowledge him. He jumps up and down begging for my attention. He is faithful. He makes me smile. He makes me happy.

Whenever a love interest comes to my house I watch closely how he responds to my dog. Right now I have a Wheaton Terrier, who is very friendly. The man does not have to love my dog like I do, but it is important to see that he can be kind to a creature that obviously needs affection.

My friend Alyssa has a small, white Bichon Frise. One day we were sharing the escapades of our pets during a phone call.

"Sometimes, I wake up in my bed with Dodger laying right next to me," I joked over the phone. "He'll be stretched out on his back, legs gapped open, and snoring like he's my man!"

Alyssa giggled. "My little one is happily sitting in my lap right now."

I took a deep breath. "You can't beat that kind of love can you?"

"Nope. This is really what I want from a man," Alyssa added. "When he comes home from a hard day at work, I will jump in his lap, and I want him to hug me, kiss me, rub my belly, and pat me on my behind."

~~~~~~

Playin' the Game

For generations women have been told in order to get a man we have to learn how to play the game. Be nice, but not too nice; act needy, but not too needy; play dumb, but not too dumb. Some of us can play the game very well and some of us can't. Of course, I fall into the latter group.

My boyfriend, years ago, would sing the praises of his best friend's girl. "Marissa would make a wonderful wife," he declared on numerous occasions. Marissa cooked like a trained chef and cleaned like a hired maid service. Sadly, he had me, and I was the total opposite of Marissa. I rarely cooked, and even though my house was decent, cleaning was not my thing. I love to eat out and I like hiring somebody to clean.

After tolerating his misplaced admiration for quite a while, I finally had to say something. We were sitting in his living room when he started in again about how wonderful Marissa was, and I exploded.

"Marissa has to play the game," I huffed. "She has to be a fabulous cook and a great maid because she's been married before. She's bringing two kids into the relationship as part of the package." I actually continued on with an embarrassing level of arrogance now that I think about it. "She didn't go to college and I'm not sure if she even finished high school, so what other choice does she have?"

It's a really bad habit of mine. I don't like to fight, so I hold stuff in and by the time I finally speak up the anger or hurt has taken over. His praise had become an insult to me as a career woman. I finished my tirade by telling him that if he wanted someone like Marissa, then he needed to go out and find her.

"I didn't get married early, and I don't have kids on purpose," I added. "I wanted a career. I have better things to do with my life than cook and clean."

Needless to say, his good friend married Marissa. Maybe a year later, my boyfriend came in after visiting their house and complained about how bad things were.

He scowled. "It was a mess. Stuff was everywhere."

There was nothing I needed to say. Marissa had played the game and won, and honestly, I wasn't mad at her. With that ring on her finger, she no longer had to cook like Rachel Ray, or clean like Molly Maids.

Comedian Steve Harvey in his book *Act Like a Lady, Think Like a Man* tells career-minded women who choose to remain strong and independent that it means they will be lonely and sad for most of their lives. He says that we have to show a man that we need him. In other words, his answer to the career women's dilemma is that she should play the role of a subservient female in order to stroke the man's ego and ultimately win his love.

To some extent, Harvey has the same problem as Tyler Perry. Rather than telling women that they should act subservient to men, he needs to help men appreciate what it means to have a strong, successful black woman in their life.

This is a woman who chooses to be with you because she wants to not because she has to. This is a woman who loves you and has your back: mentally, spiritually, physically, and financially. This is a woman who can take care of herself but wants to build a good life with you.

Maybe men could understand that a strong, successful black woman is a Godsend if they worried more about her heart and less about her accomplishments.

Steve Harvey did get one thing right in his book, I'm the prize!

~~~~~~~

Angry Black Women

Sometimes I wonder why people are surprised by black women's anger. As a matter of fact, when you think about what black women have gone through, maybe they have a right to be angry. Our ancestors sacrificed a lot to hold the black family together, yet today the black family is in bad shape. Instead of appreciating and understanding the need for strong black women, too often we're discarded, devalued, and maligned by everyone, including black men.

Sometimes, it feels like strong, independent, career-minded women in the twenty-first century, especially African American women, are being punished. Comedian D. L. Hughley said in a 2012 National Public Radio interview that black women are the angriest group of people he's ever met. Helena Andrews declared *Bitch is the new Black* in her popular memoir.

A reporter in *The Guardian* called ESPN's Jemele Hill an angry black woman when she suggested that fans should boycott the Dallas Cowboys' advertisers if they disagreed with its owner's decision to bench any player who kneeled in protest.

A *New York Times* critic suggested that successful television producer Shonda Rhimes' biography should be titled, "How to Get Away With Being an Angry Black Woman." Even the former First Lady Michelle Obama couldn't escape the stereotype whether she was shutting down a heckler, dealing with her White House aides or on the cover of *The New Yorker* dressed as a terrorist wearing a big afro, military fatigues, and combat boots.

The American Advertising Federation, Howard University, and Zeta Phi Beta Sorority established a consortium to challenge the "angry black woman" stereotype. In their 2017 survey they found that black women were most often seen in the media as argumentative, lazy, and corrupt. Only twelve percent of the respondents reported that they noticed positive images of black women in the media.

It's true, in a lot of movies and television shows the career-oriented black female character is demonized. One obvious example was the popular film *The Best Man* (1999) directed by Spike Lee's cousin Malcolm Lee. I enjoyed the film except for its problematic storyline that suggested career women like Jordan, played by Nia Long, are man-degrading, family-destroying, wannabe-lesbians who deserve to end up alone.

Throughout the movie, several male characters maligned Jordan's ambition, and by the end, all four of the male characters had someone in their lives while the career woman was all alone.

This movie also implied that there are certain kinds of women who deserve love. For instance, Morris Chestnut's character, Lance was an egotistical, unfaithful, college turned pro-athlete. He married his girlfriend Mia after she put up with his bullshit for way too many years. Mia is described in the film as the consummate mother-whore who whips up delicious, gourmet meals in minutes. Her tolerance and forgiveness are eventually rewarded with the ultimate prize a wedding ring, the big house, and the coveted title of Mrs. Lance Sullivan.

There are other women in the film who seem to deserve love. They include the girlfriend of the best man played by Sanaa Lathan. Her career is conveniently a glorified cook who wants to start her own catering business. The socially conscious attorney Murch dumps his girlfriend who is an uppity, selfish bitch to hook up with Candy, a lap dancing hoochie by night and progressive college student by day. Even the uppity, selfish bitch ends up with the cool playa at the end of this movie.

One primary message in *The Best Man* is that the kind of

woman who ultimately gets a man is the one who puts up with un-faithfulness, cooks, cleans, and can give a good lap dance. The ca-reer woman is treated like a pariah to be scorned and pitied. In the sequel to this movie the career woman has gone outside of her race to find a man.

In her 1937 book, *Their Eyes Were Watching God* Zora Neale Hurston referred to black women as the "mules of the world carrying the burdens of their race." This still feels true today. I would argue that feminism has not made those burdens lighter for black women, but increased them substantially. Although feminism brought free-dom for white women enabling them to choose between being a homemaker and working outside of the home, most African Ameri-can women were already forced to work long hours for little pay. They had no choice.

Early feminism, according to bell hooks, used the term "wom-an" to primarily mean white women, while in the Civil Rights Movement the term "black" primarily referred to black men. In her book *Ain't I a Woman?* hooks suggested that the sixties and sev-enties were difficult for black women because they were asked to support a feminist movement designed for white women, and they participated in a black movement that served the interests of the black male patriarchy.

I think we should be angry. We should be angry that we are undervalued when it comes to the ability to climb the corporate lad-der. We should be angry that we are located at the bottom of the list when it comes to good dating material. We should be angry that we earn less money than whites, Asians, and even black men. We should be angry that stress is killing us in higher numbers than any other group.

It is sad that so many people, even black men, fall into the trap of seeing black women as angry, mean or needy, and abandon us. We've all heard the rhetoric that passes for truth in American soci-ety. White women are easier to be with, more giving, and will do what they are told to do. Black women are evil, always mad about something, and they expect too much.

As a valuable legacy of our ancestors, black women fought

hard so that the black family could survive more than four hundred years of slavery, segregation, discrimination, and inequality. All we want is love, appreciation, and security. Not only do we want it, but we deserve it.

If black women are angry, maybe we have a right to be.

It's Raining Men

~~~~~~

*"Good relationships feel good. They feel right. They
don't hurt. They're not painful. That's not just with
somebody you want to marry, but it's also with the
friends that you choose."*

Michelle Obama

~~~~~~

Driven

"Driven." That was the word he used. He didn't say it in a malicious or nasty way. He wasn't sad or angry. With a nonchalant shrug, he stood up, spoke that one word, and walked out.

I remember glancing through the bedroom window into a bright, sun-filled sky that made me think briefly about going after him. I thought maybe that I should try to work things out. After all, I loved him… at least I thought I loved him… well… I really wanted to love him. Instead, I yawned without covering my mouth, crawled under the comforter on my king-sized heavenly bed, and closed my eyes.

Moments later, just before I slipped into a deep, numbing sleep, I heard the beat of an old friend, "Boom, boom, boom, another one bites the dust." Queen sang, and I hummed along.

I thought there was plenty of time. I thought there would always be lots of choices. I thought it was a simple matter of deciding when I was ready and accepting the best offer. What you want and what you get are sometimes two very different things. Ultimately, I have learned that it doesn't matter that you are holding all the right cards if everyone else is playing dominoes.

In my early years, marriage was easy to push to the back of my eight-and-a-half-by-eleven, notebook-sized to-do list. Someday, when the time was right, I would find a good guy and take that leap of faith. And then later, as I settled into my career and tried to manage my busy lifestyle, marriage and my job always seemed constantly out of sync.

The time wasn't right although the man was a good one or the man wasn't right, but it seemed like a good time to take that next step.

Sometimes, I worry that maybe I met the man that God approved for my life and somehow missed him. But, that doesn't make sense because if he truly was the man that God wanted in my life he'd be here with me, wouldn't he?

My reverend once told me that God allows us to meet a number of wrong men so that we will appreciate the right one when he finally shows up. When I asked God to send me the man that He wanted in my life, the person who showed up could not have been God's choice. I told my reverend that it didn't work and he chuckled.

"When you're praying to God you have to remember that Satan is listening too," he explained.

I would open myself up to date someone from a different race or ethnicity if the chemistry was there. Somebody like Tom Selleck in *Blue Bloods* or a taller version of my Latino physical therapist would work quite nicely. But, that doesn't mean I'm ready to give up on black men. I believe there are good black men out there and I only need to find one. The one that feeds my mind, strengthens my spirit, warms my soul, and curls my toes.

That morning after he left, I took a deep breath, closed my eyes, and sang along with Queen because what else could I do? I was driven when we met, and he knew it. He knew who and what he was getting from the first kiss. I wasn't going to change, so there was really no point in chasing after him.

"Boom, boom, boom," as the drumbeat from Queen eventually died down in my head, I welcomed the silence and slept.

~~~~~

Heaven Must be Like This

My first year living in Houston, Texas, as young people used to say, was cray cray. I had never seen so many black men in my life; tall ones, short ones, smart ones, sexy ones, funny ones, passionate ones, employed ones, unemployed ones, old ones, young ones, intelligent ones, charming ones, muscular ones, thin ones, dark ones, light ones, and everything in-between. You have to grow up in a place like Iowa to understand the thrill of seeing black couples, black families, and single black men everywhere.

I had been living in Houston for almost three months when I called my mother and told her Houston was as close to heaven as I could get and still be alive.

I moved to Houston because I wanted to live in a large city. I wanted warm weather all year round. I wanted to live near a large body of water, specifically one of the coasts. I wanted a significant black population. And, I wanted to go to pro football and basketball games.

I was naïve enough back then, to think maybe I wanted to marry a pro-athlete. It seemed like a logical path for me. When he was out on the road I could work on my career. When he was home I could spend time with him.

Meeting members of the Houston Rockets and Houston Oilers quickly changed my thinking. I was working as a news reporter, so I met athletes all the time. When I saw how ridiculous women acted around them, I knew that lifestyle would not work for me.

On a date with a Houston Rocket, while we waited for our table at a popular restaurant, some girl walked up, positioned herself between the two of us and started talking to him. Actually, she turned her back to me and began flirting obnoxiously with him. He was a gentleman. He stepped to the side, put his arm around me, and told her that I was his date. The girl did not give up. Still ignoring me, she held out a felt pen and asked for his autograph. As he reached for the pen, she flipped her long weave over her shoulder and pointed to her uncovered cleavage. He chuckled, glanced around, picked up a napkin from a nearby table and scribbled something on it. When he handed her the napkin, she turned up her nose and stormed away. I couldn't deal with that stupidity on a daily basis.

It was the early eighties and the sexual revolution was exploding. Women, just like men, had decided that sex without a commitment could be a good thing. They didn't have to be bogged down trying to make a relationship work. They were finally starting to understand that line that men throw out like Mardi Gras beads, "Sex and love are two different things."

I dated a popular media personality for a while. No dated is the wrong term, we hung out when it was convenient. This was a relationship that had absolutely nothing to do with love. This was an experience that gave me happiness, excitement, and freedom.

This was a relationship that allowed me to know all of the colors of the rainbow. His deep, sexy, purple voice was the ultimate turn on. We would sneak away from work for a golden afternoon delight, enjoy a midnight blue rendezvous or wake up to a tangerine passion morning. There were no strings attached, no commitments, no expectations, nothing beyond the amazing time we spent together.

One afternoon as we lay in each other's arms, he kissed me on my forehead and asked: "Is sex really all you want from me?"

The question was unexpected, so I didn't really take it seriously. "What else do you have to offer?" I teased.

I had entered into the relationship knowing that he was popular, charming, and good-looking. He was surrounded by lots of beautiful groupies. I liked him. I liked him a lot, but I didn't want to go through the changes that I knew would come in a serious relationship with him.

I didn't realize it then, but that was not the response he was looking for. I think he was trying to tell me that he wanted more. Sex can be a powerful connection between two people. Although you plan not to get involved or not to care it's difficult to control how you feel after joining together intimately.

I ended our connection because, truthfully, I was feeling the same way. I had realized that sex was not enough. I wanted more. I wanted intimacy. I wanted love. It was exciting to finally know what I wanted. Even better, I knew who I wanted.

~~~~~~

The Engagement Ring

Somebody gave me an engagement ring once, and if there is such a thing as a soul mate, he was probably mine. I met him in the last year of my master's program at the University of Iowa. He was a couple of years younger and finishing his final year at a small college in Iowa. He was a tall, sexy, passionate, good-looking brother. Whenever I think of him, it's his smile that comes to mind. It was his smile that won my heart.

We dated for about a year until I finished my degree and moved to Texas. That was the plan before I met him. And even though he was cute and funny and sweet, there was nothing that could have kept me in Iowa back then. As a matter of fact, I had spent my entire life trying to get out of Iowa. As I mentioned earlier, I was going to live in a big city with professional football and basketball teams. I was going to leave the cold winters for warm weather all year round. I was going to surround myself with black people and black culture.

In 1979, I did my research and came up with three top choices: Los Angeles, Houston, and Atlanta. I knew pretty quickly that Los Angeles was too big and too impersonal. People in Los Angeles seemed stressed out and superficial. Atlanta was cool with lots of potential. It met all of the criteria on my list, but it couldn't compete with Houston. From the moment I drove into Houston, Texas I was hooked. It was a big city moving at the speed of a country town, and I fit right in.

Houston had everything I wanted: a large black community, pro teams, and warm weather. But, I was most intrigued with seeing black couples everywhere. Coming from Iowa where the pickin's were slim, I was mesmerized by the variety of tall, dark, gorgeous male bodies. I already told you about that amazing experience in an earlier chapter.

What I didn't say earlier was that even though I enjoyed being surrounded by lots of black men, I missed the smile I had left behind. We talked by phone, and he visited a few times. Then he made plans to move to Houston after his graduation. For the first time in my life, I would have both a relationship and a career. I was thrilled about the future.

When he bought my engagement ring, I was convinced he was the man I would spend my life with. He loved me. He understood me. He had moved across the country to be with me. Some people think I worry too much about the little things and in some cases they might be right. But, as I thought about starting a family and being a good mother and wife, I realized that a career in radio or television news was not the right direction.

I didn't like working in the real world. I didn't like working in the middle of the night, on weekends or during holidays. I had started teaching part-time at Texas Southern University, and I noticed that the professors at the university had a much more flexible schedule. Classes could be arranged, for the most part, plus there were summer and holiday breaks.

I already had my bachelor and master degrees from Iowa, so I decided to apply for the Ph.D. program at the University of Texas in Austin. We discussed the opportunity, and he supported my decision. I would move to Austin to complete my coursework in two or three years, then come back to Houston to write my dissertation. It was only a three-hour drive, so we could travel back and forth on weekends to see each other. We would talk on the phone throughout the week. It seemed like a doable plan.

Of course, few plans work out the way you want them to. When I realized I had morning sickness a couple of months later I freaked. My life was suddenly a statistic. Only six out of one thousand women who use an IUD got pregnant.

"I'm not ready for a baby!" I remember yelling at him as soon as I entered the apartment. I was determined not to let him talk me into doing something that I did not want to do.

He didn't say anything. He let me go on and on about my career and my choices. When I was finished, he said softly: "Do what you want to do."

It was a much longer conversation than that, but I don't remember every word. What I remember is that I had already made up my mind to have an abortion and nobody could talk me out of it. It wasn't until many years later, when I held my daughter in my arms, that I understood what an empty victory I won that day.

I don't believe anyone should take away a woman's right to choose, but experiencing the awesome miracle of life makes it hard not to regret my decision. I later learned that he wanted me to keep the baby, even though he didn't say it. But, to be honest, I don't think there was anything he could have said or done at that time to change my mind.

The move to Austin went fine for the first couple of years. We talked during the week and saw each other on weekends. Since I didn't receive any fellowship money from the University of Texas, I taught full-time at Huston Tillotson College. That meant it was taking longer to complete my coursework, pass comprehensive exams, and write the dissertation proposal. I needed to be ABD (all but dissertation) in order to move back to Houston.

One weekend while visiting my fiancé in Houston, I felt like something was wrong. I could sense that we were starting to drift apart, but it was more than that. I didn't know exactly what was going on, and I became uncomfortable in his space. I had never felt uncomfortable before. I tried to ignore it during a few more trips, but eventually it was a conversation we had to have.

"Something is wrong," I began as we sat in his living room watching a movie.

He shrugged. "What are you talking about?"

"I don't know. It feels like you don't want me here."

He looked at me and frowned. "What? That's crazy."

"I'm serious. I don't feel comfortable in your apartment any more. It's hard to explain, but something has changed."

"You're trippin," he mumbled and shook his head.

"So things are okay with us?"

"As far as I'm concerned things are fine."

"And there's nothing for me to worry about?"

"Nothing that I know of."

"This is not something I'm imagining, something really does feel wrong."

"If you feel something is wrong, that's your problem, not mine," he replied sarcastically.

His last statement ripped through my mind in a continuous loop on the three-hour drive back to Austin the next day. It didn't matter that he had denied it. I knew there was something or someone wedged between us. By the time I got home, I had decided that if it was my problem, then I knew how to solve it. I had my own apartment in Austin. I felt comfortable in my apartment. So I would just stay in Austin.

I started making excuses on the weekends when I was supposed to travel to Houston. At first, it didn't seem to bother him, probably because he could do whatever he was doing in Houston and still see me on his weekends. But several months went by, and I think it finally hit him that I hadn't been there in quite a while.

I learned later that he was seeing someone else, and like most men, his guilty mind went into overdrive. Since he was stepping out, of course, I must be cheating too. One evening my neighbor and good friend saw him parked down the street in his car watching my apartment. I guess he was trying to catch me with my phantom lover. She talked him into leaving.

When she told me what happened, I knew I had to do something because I loved him and I wanted things to work out for us. I applied for and received a one-year United Methodist Fellowship that would enable me to quit teaching and concentrate on writing my dissertation. I figured I would move back to Houston and write the dissertation.

It was the mid-eighties, and the Texas oil economy had tanked, so you could literally get a two or three hundred thousand dollar house for half price. We talked about using part of my fellowship money for a down payment to buy a house. I would keep some of the money for my own personal expenses. Since I wouldn't be working, he'd have to take care of the major bills. It was a leap because I wasn't used to depending on anyone else.

My dream has always been to have a house with a swimming pool. In Houston, it seemed like every other house had a swimming pool, so I didn't think it was a big deal to look at some houses with pools. I arranged to go to Houston for several weekends in a row to look at houses with him, and I was surprised that not one of those houses had a pool. Later, when I asked why no houses had pools he said we couldn't afford it or we didn't need it, something like that. This was a huge red flag for me.

Remember, for most of my life I had watched my mother tolerate living my father's dreams rather than her own. I refused to do that. Plus, I am not good at accepting the word no. I work very hard, and if I want something, I'm going to do everything I can to get it.

Suddenly, the idea of moving back to Houston didn't seem like such a good one. I made an excuse about needing to stay in Austin, and I think this began our long road to goodbye.

The weekend when he asked for his engagement ring back, I shouldn't have been surprised, but I was. Deep down I had hoped that somehow we could fix things. I hesitated before I handed the ring to him. As he held it in his hand, my hopeful romantic emerged. I wanted him to say something like: "I don't want this ring, I want you. I love you, and I want to spend my life with you." Of course, this was not a movie and fairy tales aren't real. So he took the ring and walked out the door.

Years later, he told me that he didn't expect me to give the ring back. As a matter of fact, he didn't want me to give it back. He wanted me to say "I love you and I want to spend the rest of my life with you."

This was the one love in my life that might have had staying power. His love was as close to a real love as I would ever get. I should have fought harder to hold onto him. But, at that time in my life, I was too immature and too driven.

~~~~~~

My Baby's Daddy

I spent many years trying not to have a baby without a husband. But at thirty-six years old my biological clock lit up like fireworks on the Fourth of July, and I knew it was time. I decided to take a very practical approach to marriage. I would conduct my search for a good husband with the same focus and intensity that I had used to secure my successful career.

There was a magazine article (I don't remember which magazine) that offered five tips for finding a good man. I followed three of them. First, I told all of my friends that I was looking. Second, I didn't limit my options. I kept my range of possibilities as broad as possible. Third, I was honest up front with every man I met. I told him I was looking for a committed relationship that would lead to marriage and a couple of kids within a few years. The article included a warning that he might run when he hears the truth, but if he didn't want the same thing I wanted I didn't have time to waste.

Over about a year, I identified five possible candidates and started the interviewing process. There was a psychologist in Atlanta; a journalist from New Orleans; a photographer from Louisville; a musician in Philadelphia; and a doctor from Detroit. I talked on the phone to all of them for hours, in order to learn as much as I could. Eventually, I narrowed it down to three and visited each of them. The article said it was important to check out their lifestyle.

The doctor from Detroit quickly rose to the top. He said everything I wanted to hear, and it didn't hurt that he was one of the best lovers I have ever had. His mother worked, so he said that he had no problem with career women. I was honest and told him up front that cooking every night was not my thing, plus I expected everyone to pitch in when it came to cleaning. He said he could deal with that.

We dated long distance for a year until he moved to Iowa and started a residency at the university hospital. Six months later I was pregnant. We both wanted a child, so the baby was not an accident. We were excited. I moved my office out of the second bedroom upstairs and decorated that room in yellows, reds, and browns. Nine months later, my beautiful baby girl was born.

Everything was happening so fast that I found myself ignoring the red flags that were popping up. For example, we argued about cooking greens, making up the bed, and cleaning the bathroom. I started to notice that some of the things he had said during our courtship were not matching up with what he was doing now that we were living together.

Once our daughter was born, I went back to teaching and writing, so I was spread very thin. The cleaning system we had before the baby was not working. To be fair, he did stuff like washed his clothes and the baby's clothes, took out the trash, and mowed the lawn.

One day when I asked about hiring a cleaning person a couple of times a month because I just couldn't get it all done. He said no. At this point, the dust on the bookshelves was a quarter inch thick, I couldn't remember the last time the rug had been vacuumed, and the upstairs bathroom needed some serious attention.

"We don't need to do that," he grumbled.

"Well, I can't do it. I don't have time. I have the baby and work."

"It only takes thirty minutes to clean the bathroom."

I remember those words clearly because the hair on the back of my neck stood up.

"You don't get it," I told him. "If I have an extra thirty minutes I don't want to spend it cleaning the bathroom. I want to spend it playing with the baby, or writing my next novel, or watching my favorite television show."

"Well, I don't want a stranger in the house going through our things," he barked.

"Then you can do it," I snapped back. "Because I can't."

"Okay fine, I'll do it," he said.

A week went by with no cleaning and, eventually, the upstairs bathroom was in such bad shape that the baby and I started using the downstairs one. By the end of the month, he still had not done anything, so I called a cleaning service and set up a time for them to come.

My baby's daddy is a good guy. He just wasn't the right guy for me. What I learned from him is that a lot of professional men claim they want a career woman, but in reality what they want is a woman with a job. They want somebody who goes to work, brings home a paycheck, but someone who still cooks, cleans, takes care of the kids, and screws on a regular basis.

We had talked about marriage on several occasions before he moved to Iowa. And I had shared with him ahead of time that I didn't want to have a baby without a husband. He assured me that wouldn't happen. But, once I was pregnant he admitted that he didn't think it was a good idea for us to get married. He said we had some issues we needed to figure out. I agreed.

I think my mother took it much harder than I did. She's still old-fashioned even though she tries to be hip. Her first child had done all of these great things: earned a Ph.D., written a bestselling novel, and bought her first house. Mom couldn't accept the fact that I was going to be one of those women who had a baby without being married. I felt bad too, I was going to be a stereotype, but there was nothing I could do about it.

My first novel *So Good, An African American Love Story* was published in 1996 by Dutton/Penguin, the same year that my daughter was born. The excitement of seeing my first novel in bookstores was a wonderful experience. And, once I got past hours of labor and childbirth without drugs, holding my beautiful daughter in my arms was even better.

It was an article in *Essence* magazine that turned out to be my saving grace. The phone interview with one of *Essence's* editors took about thirty minutes. We mainly talked about the story and the characters, but at the very end, she asked me a couple of questions concerning my personal life. I told her that I disagreed with those people who say forty is downhill because I was about to turn forty, I was pregnant with my first child, living with my fiancé, and publishing my first novel. Life was very good.

When the article came out it was like a huge burden was lifted off of my back because the world now knew that I was pregnant without a husband. I stopped worrying and started celebrating!

A Train Ride to Boston

I once had an imaginary relationship with a man for almost four years. And, truth be told, it was almost as good as some of my real relationships. I know how crazy that sounds, but it's true. We were part of a Bid Whist club, and we played cards every Friday night. Through rain, snow, sleet, and hail we were as faithful as the person who delivers the mail.

Playing cards with this man was, in my mind, practically the same as dating him. The Bid Whist games were our dates. We flirted and laughed and teased and touched all through the night. Dealing the cards was a sensual experience, playing as his partner was true romance, the excitement of winning a game together was all about foreplay, and the ecstasy of sending our opponents on a train ride to Boston was like having a virtual orgasm.

I love the game of Bid Whist. Other games like Spades, War, Dirty Hearts, Crazy Eights, Solitaire, Poker or Blackjack can't compare. I especially loved playing Bid Whist with this man. I've watched him bid a six-no-trump with very little in his hand and somehow make it. He explained to me several times that he was bidding not only on his hand, but also on the six-card kitty, and what his partner might have. I couldn't do it.

Playing Bid Whist with him was like dancing an exotic dance. There was a rhythm that linked us together. We understood the strategies of the game in the same way that a couple understands how to move together in a tango. There was a level of comfort and familiarity in our partnership. Playing the right cards at the right time was the same as dancing in sync. The seductive nature of the game felt almost as good as being tangled in each other's arms.

I am usually pretty aggressive when I decide I want a certain man in my life, but with him it was different. I never really went after him like I normally would have. Maybe I thought if it was meant to be it would happen naturally. Maybe I was waiting for him to approach me first. Maybe I wasn't sure he felt the same way.

We became good friends over the years, and that meant a lot to me during that time in my life. One night I got a phone call from the wife of the guy I was talking to long distance. I was devastated. The liar had told me that he was divorced. Of course, he never wore a ring when we were together.

I called my Bid Whist friend that night very upset, and he invited me over. He allowed me to vent for hours about trifling men, and how much relationships suck. He offered me food and drink. He let me cry on his shoulder and held me in his arms until I fell asleep.

I thought maybe we had turned the corner that night, but at the next Bid Whist game we picked up exactly where we left off. Our opponents were challenged to take out his bid of five uptown.

"No guts, no glory," our opponent taunted, but his partner passed anyway. My partner won the bid. After choosing hearts as his trump, we worked closely together to make the bid. After laying down the final winning card, he winked at me.

I've heard that people come into your life for specific reasons and seasons. I think maybe he was important during that period of my life because he allowed me to focus on my writing and publishing. By the time I came up for promotion and tenure everything was in place. My research, my teaching and my service were solid, so I was easily promoted from assistant to associate professor with tenure.

~~~~~~

Tired Black Men

If I hear another black man say he is tired I'm going to go ballistic. If black men are tired, what the hell do they think black women are? We are bone weary, worn-out, drained, and downright exhausted.

Tim Alexander's 2008 independent film *Diary of a Tired Black Man* suffered from its own title. Alexander broke down the complexity of a relationship into a one-sided misrepresentation of black women's fear. In other words, from the male character's perspective all black women are angry.

The movie actually made me think about a place down in Plano, Texas called the Cockroach Hall of Fame. On display was every kind of roach you could imagine. From the small German two-striped and the Oriental wingless to the mahogany colored water bug and the huge winged Palmetto. Someone who apparently didn't have a life created several displays suggesting the existence of a parallel roach society. In one glass case there was a roach relaxing at the beach. A thin layer of sand had been spread under a tiny, striped, towel-looking piece of fabric. On top of the fabric, the Oriental cockroach was laying comfortably shaded by one of those cute little umbrellas that comes with a tropical drink. In another display, a flying Palmetto modeled a blue, silk dress on a beauty pageant runway made from a painted cardboard box. And, finally, a Liberace roach was wrapped in white fur and sitting behind a toy baby grand piano painted gold.

I know it is unfair to compare all black men to roaches, the same way it is unfair to suggest that all black women are angry. We need to be careful about the stereotypes we perpetuate when it comes to black culture.

There are things that black men should be tired of like:

-dying at the hands of other black men and the police.
-confirming the stigma of thugs, criminals, and gang-
    bangers with their pants hanging off their butts.
-seeing the first black president of the United States
    be disrespected.
-allowing black children to grow up in poverty and be
    denied a good education.
-spending money on stupid stuff like expensive cars,
    gold chains, platinum or diamond teeth.
-accepting the stereotypes of pimps, playas, hoochies,
    and hoes.

In 2006, I couldn't help but scream when the rap song "It's Hard out Here for a Pimp" from the movie *Hustle and Flow* was given an Oscar for best original song. I don't know what the voters were thinking. There was nothing special about that song. It sounded like a hundred other rap songs. It had the same repetitive beat, words, and rhyming style. That award gave legitimacy to a very problematic stereotype in black culture, pimps and pimpin'.

The fact that this ridiculous song was chosen over more positive and powerful nominations made me question the academy's decision even more. From *Crash*, a great movie, the theme song "In the Deep" talked about how people are tumbling, spinning, and swimming through difficult lives. The song "Travelin' Thru" by Dolly Parton in the movie *Transamerica* explored the need for redemption, the puzzle of life's journey, and the joy of going home.

During the Academy Awards ceremony the performance of "It's Hard Out Here for a Pimp" by Three 6 Mafia was really embarrassing. It glorified negative images of black culture with rappers imitating pimps and hustlers while black women strutted around on stage shaking their behinds dressed like streetwalkers and prostitutes.

I have talked with students in my classes about how movies like *Hustle and Flow* present specific images and messages about culture and society. I want them to understand how the audience often buys into the images and messages when they are intertextual and repetitive. So, when the audience supports DJay's dream of becoming a rap star, on some level, they begin to accept what DJay is doing to the three girls in his stable: the pregnant Shug, Nola who turns tricks in an alley, and his strip club hoe Lexus.

Too many videos, movies, and films normalize butt-shaking hoochie mamas and gang-banging baby daddies. Those problematic images and messages that promote ignorance and glamorize negativity concerning black culture is what black men should be tired of. As a matter of fact, we all need to understand how powerful and persuasive those images and messages are around the world.

One thing I know for sure, a concept borrowed from Oprah and O Magazine, it is harder out here for an intelligent, successful, career-oriented, black woman than it is for a damn pimp.

~~~~~~

Peace My Sister

If I had to choose one thing that is crucial for a good relationship it would be communication. I think author John Gray got it right when he characterized men and women's communication styles as being from two different planets: Mars and Venus. I have dated wonderful men whose inability to communicate eventually destroyed any possibilities. I believe if two people can't talk on a meaningful level it is hard, maybe even impossible, to build a relationship that lasts.

There was one guy who was supposed to be interested in me. We lived in different states. I would maybe hear from him once a week. I tried to explain that since the relationship was long distance we needed to connect more by phone. No change. The man did not own a cell phone, and I could not convince him to get one. It was not a relationship that I could make work, so I had to shut it down.

Even worse are those guys who start out calling every day, three times a day, and then once you have those expectations they change. What is that line? The same thing you do to get someone you have to do if you want to keep them.

A retired attorney that I dated for a while seemed to be a great match. Everything was going well until he decided to start practicing law again. We had talked about his frustration with this country's justice system. This led him to retire in the first place. Once he started taking the necessary continuing education courses our relationship was over.

The man went from calling two or three times a day, every day, to not calling or answering my calls over a week or more. Then one day, I received a brief text message that said something like: "Sorry, been here before."

I have never really liked roller-coaster rides. When I was younger, I would get on them because that was the thing to do, but now that I'm older no thank you. I went on a roller-coaster ride in Harry Potter World at Universal Studios with my daughter and two of her friends a few years ago. I quickly remembered that this was an experience I would rather do without. My eyes were closed for most of the ride, especially when the cart was about to drop suddenly. My stomach twisted into knots and my heart felt like it was going to pound out of my chest. It was not what I call fun.

My relationship with the retired attorney was like a roller-coaster ride. In the beginning, I wasn't sure I was even interested. He wasn't what I was looking for, but he seemed like such a nice guy. I admit that I put him through a few hoops because I wanted to be sure, and finally when I decided to commit the man was gone.

Of course, I analyzed the situation to death with my friends, and we came up with some interesting ideas. One suggestion was that everything is tied to the "male ego," so he was probably intimidated by my success. I don't buy that. This man was an attorney. He was intelligent and confident. He had absolutely no reason to be intimidated by me.

Another friend thought maybe he had gotten too close too quickly and it scared him. But, I don't know if that works either. We weren't teenagers embarking on our first love. We were both over fifty. Age is supposed to bring maturity – right?

Finally, a male psychologist friend offered a possible explanation that blew me away. He told me the minute the man decided that where he was in his life was not good enough our relationship was over.

I cocked my head to the side like a confused puppy. "I never felt that way, and I didn't tell him that he wasn't good enough," I retorted.

"It is not about what you said," my friend shrugged, and then continued. "It was something he felt, and there was nothing you could have said or done that would have made a difference."

Now I was frowning. His words connected.

"In that kind of situation," he continued. "If you respond positively to the decision he might feel something like: 'She doesn't appreciate me for who I am.' Or if you respond negatively with: 'You don't need to do that. You're fine just the way you are,' he might think: 'She doesn't support my dreams.'"

One good thing that came out of that relationship was my improved technological ability. When we met I didn't text. Since he liked to text, I had to learn how to do it. Unfortunately, it also meant I would experienced my first breakup by text message. Welcome to the world of millennials.

At first, when he stopped communicating I tried to leave the door open. I thought whatever the problem is maybe it can be solved. But, after a couple of months of hoping it was him every time the phone rang, I knew I had to close the door and move on.

I sent a text message. Sometimes we would tease each other about being playas in our younger days. My text joked:

"Bravo Playa, it was an outstanding performance."

He responded, "Huh?"

I clarified. "If the purpose was to see if you've still got it, you do."

"If you're saying what I think you're saying then my opinion of you was probably too high," he replied.

I paused for a minute and typed, "Unfortunately, I've already come to the same conclusion." I pressed enter.

He sent back, "Peace my sister."

I replied, "Go to hell, my brother."

Wait a minute. I guess I have to be honest. I did type that last line, but I never sent it.

When I told my psychologist friend about our last text exchange, he looked at me incredulously.

"What other response did you expect?" He asked.

He went on to explain that my text was probably seen as a challenge, so of course the man was going to respond negatively.

But, I don't think I did anything wrong. My text did exactly what it was designed to do. It brought closure to the situation.

I always close my eyes on roller coaster rides as the cart drops, but even if you don't look the fear is still there.

~~~~~~

SweetChocolate

The first time I tried an online dating service it was a rush. I've met some people and heard about others who have had success meeting someone this way, so I figured why not. I googled the suggested site and skimmed the home page that said: "Welcome to Soul Singles join now!"

I clicked on the join now icon and a questionnaire appeared. The first box asked for my name. I typed in Venise Berry. Next, I typed my email name: Serpentine. Then age: fifty. I had to stop for a minute. It was hard to believe I was really fifty-years-old. After a deep breath, I continued by typing my career field, education, height, and finally email address.

I hesitated when I got to the box where my body type was requested. The choices were petite, athletic, average, and full-figured. I wanted to mark the average box because that's where I see myself. However, I know that society sees me differently. So I marked the full-figured box accepting the fact that it would probably mean a decrease in interested men. There are some men who are superficial and will not consider a beautiful, full-figured woman.

Internet dating sites used to be stigmatized as only for geeks and weirdos, but now everybody seems to be doing it. I told one of my good friends, who has dated online consistently, that I was planning to give it a try and she gave me a great tip. She said don't be cheap. Anyone can join a free site, and that means there are a lot of losers to sort through. In other words, if they are willing to pay they are probably more serious candidates.

Clicking on the finish icon, I smiled when the box with the phrase "Welcome to Soul Singles" popped up. From the main menu, I found my way into the search mode and looked at various male profiles. I took a few minutes to identify specific areas of interest like age range between forty and sixty; education at least college; and height six foot or taller. After pressing the return button forty-six profiles emerged.

I was pleasantly surprised at the large number until I looked more closely. I deleted over a third just based on names alone. They had used tired and offensive names like partypimp, slickdaddy, nastynick, thetongue or maddplayer. In my opinion, these names screamed loser, loser, freak, freak, loser.

I cut another third while laughing out loud based on the photos. Many of the pictures were blurred, too far away, too close, too dark, too light, and in several the top of the head was cut off. They also had photos with women standing behind them, next to them, sitting in their laps, and a few even had the nerve to upload a picture where the woman had been obviously cut out of the shot!

Finally, skimming the sixteen profiles that were left, only two stood out. The first came from someone calling himself Southern Breeze. He wrote: "I'm looking for a woman who is worthy of a great love. No clinging vines (get a life); no teenie boppers (get a grip); no control freaks (get a dog); no religious zealots (get a bible); and no hoochie mamas (get a clue). If you think you can handle the intensity of the love I'm offering holla back."

I didn't think I couldn't handle all that, so I didn't holla back. The second was from a cutie pie called SweetChocolate. He wrote: "I'm looking for a woman who knows what she wants, someone I can love and grow old with. We can listen to good music, eat soul food, and enjoy vacations in the Caribbean. I am a good man and I want a good woman."

I didn't even have to think about it. I clicked on the mingle mailbox to send him a quick note.

"Hey, SweetChocolate. I'm a good woman who knows what she wants. I like good music, soul food, and vacations in the Caribbean too. I also love chocolate. Let's talk."

I stared at the screen for a moment before pressing send. Despite the excitement mixed with anxiety that I felt, I have to admit it was fun to think about meeting somebody new.

Life Goes On...

~~~~~~

*"I know who I am. I am not perfect. I am not
the most beautiful woman in the world.
But I am one of them."*

Mary J. Blige

~~~~~~

Black Love in a Big White House

In January of 2009, the first black president of the United States of America and his family moved into the big white house on Pennsylvania Avenue. At that moment, Barack and Michelle Obama became powerful role models for black love. Like most African Americans in this country, I never thought we would have a black man as president in my lifetime. But, even better, President Obama is a black man who loves and is married to a strong, educated, independent, career-oriented black woman.

I framed my HOPE sign from the first campaign, and when I look at it on my wall I remember that Barack and Michelle have shown us how beautiful black love can be. I will always be thankful for the positive love that President Obama showed for his family, his culture, and his country.

How amazing is it that a black man was elected president of the United States of America, not once but twice. I caucused for Barack Obama in Iowa and voted for him in both presidential elections. I can't tell you how many times I've complained about the choices when it came to the politicians running for office. So when I had the chance to support a politician with intelligence, compassion, and confidence, one who also happened to be black, there was no hesitation.

Despite the ignorance and disrespect that many conservatives demonstrated, I cherished his tenure in the nation's top office. You had to admire this man as he calmly maneuvered through those slanderous comments and negative actions on a daily basis. Ignoring Tea Party and alt-right chatter, President Obama proved himself an excellent leader. No matter what congressional bullshit he had to wade through, he moved full force, head held high, and shoulders straight. This country will never be the same.

There is nothing more amazing than a confident black man, except maybe a confident black man who loves a black woman. After more than twenty years of marriage, Barack Obama still calls Michelle the love of his life and his best friend.

In his 2006 book *The Audacity of Hope* Obama wrote that Michelle is "funny, smart, and thoroughly charming." In various interviews, he bragged about Michelle saying she's remarkable. His aides also reported on numerous occasions that he quoted the First Lady in Oval Office meetings.

Michelle's love for Barack was also obvious. In a 2012 speech at Morgan State University, the First Lady explained why she fell in love with her husband:

> "I want the young people to pay attention
> because, see, back when I first met Barack,
> and we started dating he had everything going
> for him. All right ladies, listen to this. This
> is what I want you to be looking for. Yes, he
> was handsome — still is. I think so. He was
> charming, talented, and oh-so smart, truly.
> But that is not why I married him. Now see,
> I want the fellas to pay attention to this. You
> all listening? What truly made me fall in love
> with Barack Obama was his character. You
> hear me? It was his character. It was his
> decency, honesty, compassion, and conviction."

Even members of the press noticed the couple's loving connection. For example, Andrew Romano on *MSNBC* observed:

"... I think it's the Obamas' willingness to act in public much how they act in private —open, informal, flirtatious—that has incited most of the swooning. At the Youth Ball, I noticed the president do something that's impossible to imagine any of his predecessors doing: resting his head, eyes closed, on Michelle's shoulder."

For those who felt the need to ask that ridiculous question, was President Barack Obama black enough? My answer is absolutely yes. He comes from an African father, and he married an educated black woman. Blackness is not about the color of the skin, but about the passion of the heart.

Clarence Thomas replaced Thurgood Marshall in the Supreme Court in 1991. They are both black men when it comes to skin color, but they have very different hearts. Hopefully, black people have learned that painful lesson. We insisted that a black man replace Thurgood Marshall, but we didn't specify the nature of that black man's heart. Clarence Thomas is the complete opposite of Thurgood Marshall when it comes to beliefs, values, and attitude. It was a serious loss for America.

Barack Obama's heart can be seen in his decision to work as a community organizer for Chicago's South Side. After law school, he served as a civil rights activist rather than heading off to Wall Street. His started an initiative to help young black men reach their full potential. The organization, My Brother's Keeper has become a significant part of the Obama Foundation.

When Trayvon Martin, an unarmed black boy, was murdered in Florida, Obama said, "Trayvon Martin could have been me thirty-five years ago." This was a powerful reflection coming from the first black president in the United States of America. As president, his devotion was always to the lower income bracket of our country. He tried to improve the lives of those who faced problems such as: the lack of health care, an inadequate minimum wage, equal pay for women, legal and social injustice, as well as the attack on voting rights.

It was obvious that there were certain white people who didn't support President Obama, but I was dumbfounded when prominent black people like Tavis Smiley and Cornel West came out against him. It didn't make sense. Instead of blaming President Obama why not help him fight back against the Republicans who were undermining his authority? If they had helped to draw attention to the Republican "Congress of no," maybe they could have helped push legislators to do the right thing.

Rather than starting a campaign against the GOP who blocked all of Obama's efforts to get anything done, Smiley and West made snide comments like: "He's a Rockefeller Republican in blackface," and "He's the black mascot of the Wall Street oligarchs." They made a joke about Al Sharpton saying he couldn't be critical because he was living on Obama's plantation.

Imagine how much more President Obama may have accomplished if prominent black leaders like Tavis Smiley and Cornell West would have used their national and international platforms to help fight against the GOP's obstruction. How ridiculous is it that the Republicans voted more than fifty times to end Obamacare (the Affordable Care Act). This program helped more than twenty million poor people of all colors get access to health insurance, many for the first time. Sadly, they tried to eliminate it, and had nothing to replace it with.

Maybe West and Smiley could have led the charge for infrastructure jobs, student loan relief, raising the minimum wage, giving equal pay to women, stopping corporations from receiving tax breaks while sending jobs overseas, and securing the Buffett rule to make sure millionaires pay a tax rate comparable to the middle class.

It hurt to watch these two powerful black men fighting another powerful black man rather than the real enemy. It seems African Americans have spent so many years in the wilderness, they don't know the promised land when they are standing in the middle of it.

Despite a mixed heritage, President Obama has embraced

his blackness. From his inspirational race speech during the campaign to his connection with slain young, black men like Trayvon Martin and Mike Brown, President Obama lifted himself above the ignorance and negativity.

When I think about the kind of black man I am looking for he would definitely be at the top of my list. As a matter of fact, on my top five list would be Barack Obama, Denzel Washington, Colin Powell, Neil deGrasse Tyson, and of course Idris Elba. These are all confident and gifted black men with an intellect and swagger that displays true black power.

But, let me get back to the wonderful black couple that lived in the big white house on Pennsylvania Avenue for eight fabulous years. The first black president and his first lady offered inspiration and courage to all of us who HOPE for real love. It was an honor to share the way they laughed together, the way he looked at her, the way she touched him, the way they moved on the dance floor, and so much more.

Barack and Michelle Obama, their children Malia and Sasha, plus pets Bo and Sunny helped the world understand that African American culture is more than a stereotype. It is positive, dynamic, and resilient. Because of the Obama family, African American culture took a huge leap forward, and there is no way that anybody can change their impact on this society and the world.

Whenever I think back on the huge HOPE sign that stood in my backyard for almost a year I smile. No one who drove down the major boulevard behind my house could miss it. The brilliance of that sign when the eastern sun hit it just right in the morning always brought a smile to my face. It is the same smile that comes every time I think about the fact that we did it! During my lifetime, America put a black family in the big white house on Pennsylvania Avenue for not one, but two terms.

~~~~~~

My Heavenly Bed

The first time I stayed at a Westin Hotel I fell in love, with the bed. It was king sized, soft, and very luxurious. I sank down into the plush mattress with my head cushioned by four lavish pillows. I immersed myself in the six-hundred thread count, Egyptian cotton sheets. It felt good, really good.

Today, I'm able to experience the miracle of my own "Heavenly Bed" every night because I bought one. Because of my heavenly bed I know what true love is all about. It offers me peace no matter what else is going on in my life. It molds itself around my body, caressing me gently, and calming my soul. My "Heavenly Bed" lulls me into a sense of wonderful comfort relieving the stress of a hard day.

After that experience at the Westin, I went online to order the mattress and boxed springs. This was several months before a scheduled hysterectomy. I decided that I wanted to recuperate from my surgery in that kind of tranquility.

It was a difficult time in my life. I was losing the most important part of my womanhood. The part of me that was designed to bring life into the world. Like many others, I worried that it might make me less of a woman. I wondered if I would feel empty once it was gone.

When I think about the bizarre situation that triggered my surgery I have to laugh. One morning, sitting on the toilet I reached down to wipe and noticed that something was hanging from my vaginal opening. There was no pain, but I freaked anyway. Like Chicken Little, I started screaming because something was definitely falling. I got dressed quickly and headed straight over to my doctor's office.

After the examination, my doctor announced that I had a prolapsed uterus. I had never heard of such a thing, but apparently, my uterus just said: "Fuck it I'm out!" It literally gave up and let go. I searched the Internet to better understand what was happening and soon realized that it wasn't an unusual condition at all.

There were a number of websites and blogs offering interesting information about this phenomenon. Dr. Keith Downing wrote a journal article on the topic for *Obstetrics and Gynecology International*. In his research, he found that during the medieval period the prolapsed uterus was thought to have a life of its own like "an animal inside an animal." Medicine men would poke it with a red-hot iron to scare it back into place. Thank God for modern day medicine!

Richard Freidman and Shawna Dolansky in their book *The Bible Now* suggested that some religious scholars believed a prolapsed uterus or the swelling of a woman's womb without the husband's seed meant she had been unfaithful. This can be found in the Hebrew case of "Sotah" or the King James story of "Bathsheba."

I read on the Food and Drug Administration website that the FDA has approved several versions of a pelvic floor muscle trainer to help build uterus strength and resistance. There are several types available including silicone elongated egg-like devices that vibrate, bio-feedback monitoring devices, smartphone and Bluetooth sensors, electrotherapy stimulators, and vaginal cones.

I also saw a lot of jokes about it: "Please help, uterus falling out," "Live Chat: How to keep your female parts from deserting you," "Feminism prolapsed my uterus," and "Kegel exercises and Ben Wa Balls can help the uterus hang in there."

It has been a number of years since my surgery. I'm still a vibrant and wonderfully sexual woman. As a matter of fact, to some extent, there is a sense of relief. I can honestly say I don't miss the pain and mess of my monthly period. Plus, sex is a different experience when you don't have to worry about pregnancy, even though sexually transmitted diseases and HIV/AIDS should still be feared.

Of course, along with the good also came some bad. A major problem I've had to deal with after the surgery is full-blown menopause. Everything hit all at once: the hot flashes, night sweats, fatigue, memory lapses, increased anxiety, and mood changes. Anyone who has dealt with menopause is probably nodding right now. Research suggests that we follow in our mother's pattern. My mother has dealt with menopause off and on for more than twenty years, and she also had a "prolapsed uterus." Thanks, mom!

Anyway, back to my "Heavenly Bed." It is truly wonderful. I can't adequately describe the happiness it brings me. When I get home from work, crawling under the covers is the most amazing sensation. When I go out of town, I can't wait to get back to my own little piece of heaven (unless I'm staying in a Westin Hotel). I love having my own "Heavenly Bed" to come home to. I can depend on my "Heavenly Bed." It is always waiting for me. It loves to hold me. It makes me feel good. And it has never disappointed me. What more can a girl ask for?

~~~~~~

Jouissance

Jouir is French and it means, "enjoy." The extended word jouissance is defined by Merriam Webster as "delight, ecstasy, sexual pleasure or orgasm." Jouissance is so amazing that relationships are bound by it and babies are born from it. I was sixteen-years-old the first time I had an orgasm. My cousin Darleen had come to Iowa to visit. She was more experienced than I was, and she convinced me that I needed to get to know my body.

"You have to take care of yourself because men are gonna get theirs," Darleen insisted.

She was right. Women should know what they like and don't like. What makes them feel good and what doesn't. What leaves them satisfied and what pisses them off.

After Darleen left that summer, I took her advice. I started to explore those delicate places that were previously considered off limits. It took a while to figure things out, but when I did wow! I can still remember the first time that fire blasted through my body. I tensed up and moaned as quietly as I could. Suddenly, I understood the "lunacy" that attaches itself to many of God's creatures when it comes to sex. The power, the passion, the release, the satisfaction of jouissance can be as addictive as any drug.

In *The Color Purple*, even though Mister was married to Celie, he was visited several times by Shug, the love of his life. During one visit, Celie told Shug that she didn't like having sex with Mister because it felt like he just got on top of her and did his business. Shug laughed and called Celie a virgin. She later showed Celie what an orgasm was and after that both Mister and Celie looked forward to Shug's visits.

Darleen warned me that even though they might pretend they know what to do for a woman during sex a lot of guys don't.

"Men are not mind readers so you have to tell them what you want, but not in the heat of passion." Darleen explained one day. "It's impossible to talk to a man about what you want or need when they're focused on themselves. They'll take it the wrong way and get insulted."

When we were growing up, Darleen was ahead of her time. I remember when she pulled a package of Trojan condoms out of her purse. She said she always carried them with her just in case. It surprised me because back then carrying condoms was something only men did. She had me on the floor laughing one time when we were listening to the radio, and "Do it all Night" by Prince came on. Darleen swore that a guy didn't know what he was doing if it took all night! Another time she had a major reaction to a news story on television about somewhere in Africa or the Middle East where genital mutilation was being practiced on women. It made her so mad that she kicked over a chair.

"They only do that because they don't want women to know what satisfaction is," she hissed. "Women who can't have an orgasm can't assess a man's true potential in bed."

Later, I read about genital mutilation and learned that in some male-dominated cultures a woman's sexuality is feared. One way to control women is to eliminate their ability to have an orgasm. It is apparently a ritual that cuts and sometimes removes parts of female genitalia. This mutilation is culturally justified or it is considered a religious tradition. It takes place before puberty marking a girl's transition into womanhood. In other words, they take away the possibilities before she knows what they are.

A 2014 article in *The Guardian* called genital mutilation the violation of a girl's human rights. They said it is based on problematic social beliefs about power, women's inferiority, and sexual behavior. In a recent bulletin, the World Health Organization argues that the process has no health benefits and does nothing to maintain virginity. In other words, it is simply a way to limit a woman's sexual joy and desire, her jouissance.

During a difficult point in my life I was prescribed a depression medication. After using one brand for about a month, my doctor asked me how things were going. I had to be honest, so I leaned in close and whispered: "Things are even worse. At least when I'm depressed, and I don't have a man I can make myself happy. With this medication that's all gone."

My doctor laughed and said maybe we should try something else. I had seen two different Cymbalta commercials on television. One claimed to help with depression and the other talked about easing pain. I was experiencing both problems. I had depression and my knees ached. However, listening to the possible side effects made me hesitate. Was I willing to exchange my depression and knee pain for other possible problems like diabetes, glaucoma, yellow skin or eyes, itching, dizziness, high blood pressure, headaches, memory loss, fever, nausea, dry mouth, fatigue, liver issues, or increased bleeding?

I held off as long as I could, but eventually I tried it. I have to give Cymbalta a shout out because the pain in my knees felt better, my anxiety and depression stabilized, plus I could get happy again all by myself.

According to a 2013 *Huffington Post* article orgasms offer a number of positive health results. For example, they relieve stress, strengthen focus, cut down on insomnia, alleviate pain, curb depression, keep skin looking younger, stimulate the brain, and even help extend life. Rutgers University researchers found that orgasms are better than crossword puzzles for our brains. In the report, they called it a miracle solution to aging!

This brings me back to an earlier issue. How do we reconcile this gift of perfect pleasure that God gave us with religions that say it is only to enjoy if we are married. Even though masturbation is not cited directly in the *Bible*, some say it is included under sexual immorality. The term sexual immorality is very subjective. It can include a broad range of issues depending on who is making the judgment call. A good example is former President

Bill Clinton saying: "I did not have 'sexual relations' with that woman." The concept of sexual relations is too broad. If the president had been more specific and said what he really meant "sexual intercourse," maybe he would not have been impeached.

We live in a sex-crazed society and just saying no is not as easy as it sounds. What happens the minute you tell somebody they can't have something? They want it even more. So when the church tells young people and single people to be abstinent many try it anyway and like it.

It is difficult not to question the all or nothing perspective in Christianity. Some people wonder if there is room for moderation or compromise. For example, if you are not an alcoholic is it wrong to have a couple of drinks at a social function? Gambling can be an addiction with some people losing everything, but is it wrong to go to the casino a few times a year or play a monthly game of cards? Is the gift of jouissance really sexual immorality or can we enjoy this personal gift from God every now and then?

I had a long discussion with a close Christian friend about this topic. She believes that Christian women should choose joy over happiness because joy is spiritual and forever, while happiness is carnal and temporary. From her perspective, joy comes from an intimate sexual connection between a committed husband and wife while happiness is found in the corporeal, sexual release between two people who are just hanging out.

Obviously, most Christian women, most women, in general, would choose joy, but it takes two. When I was younger I could wait, but now in the prime of life, I'm tired of waiting. I waited years to buy my dream house hoping I would connect with the right man, and we could buy it together. At fifty years, I had to stop waiting. I bought my dream house and I'm happy in it.

Different people look at things from different perspectives and they also approach situations from different angles. Certain terms can have many meanings bringing forth a variety of choices. I wondered how the *Bible* explained joy and happiness.

In the *Bible,* the feeling of joy is described under a variety of circumstances such as, Proverbs 17:22 "A joyful heart is good medicine;" Psalms 30:5 "You may weep at night but joy comes in the morning;" Psalms 100:1 "Make a joyful noise unto the Lord;" Nehemiah 8:10 "And do not be grieved, for the joy of the Lord is your strength;" James 1:2 "Count it all joy;" Romans 15:13 "May the God of hope fill you with joy and peace in believing;" John 16:24 "Ask, and you will receive that your joy may be full;" And, Galatians 5:22 "But the fruit of the spirit is love, joy, peace, patience, kindness, goodness, and faithfulness;"

The term happiness is also prominent in the *Bible*. Examples include: Deuteronomy 33:29 "O thy happiness, O Israel, who is like thee? A people saved by Jehovah;" Ester 9:17 "They rested on the fourteenth day and made it a day for banqueting and happiness;" Job 36:11 "If they serve Him obediently, they will end their days in prosperity and their years in happiness;" Psalms 32:1 "O the happiness of him whose transgression is forgiven, whose sin is uncovered;" Psalms 146:5 "O the happiness of him who hath the God of Jacob for his help, his hope is on Jehovah his God;" And, Proverbs 29:17 "Discipline your child and He will give you rest, He will bring you happiness;"

It is important to note that the *Bible* also combines joy and happiness in several versus like Jeremiah 15:16 "As Your words came to me I drank them in, and they filled my heart with joy and happiness because I belong to You;" Luke 1:14 "And you will have joy and happiness and many people will rejoice when He is born;" Esther 8:17 "Throughout every province and throughout every city where the king's edict and his law arrived, the Jews experienced happiness and joy, banquets and holidays;" Isaac 35:10 "They will enter Zion with a happy shout, unending joy will crown them, happiness and joy will overwhelm them; grief and suffering will disappear;" And, Jeremiah 31:13 "I will turn their mourning into joy, give them consolation and bring happiness out of grief."

Maybe someday I'll have a husband in order to experience divine joy. In the meantime, I can't fill my heart with regret worrying about what I don't have. All I can do is live my life embracing the happiness that comes with what I do have.

~~~~~~

Proverbial Wisdom

American: "You can't judge a book by its cover."
Chinese: "Rotten wood cannot be carved."
African: "Quarrels end, but words once spoken never die."
Spain, Italy, Germany, Scotland: "Better to bend than break."
Chinese: "Man who fight with wife all day gets no
          peace/piece at night."
Tanzania, Kenya, Mozambique and the Congo:
          "Don't throw away the fish or you may regret when
          someone else picks it up."
Ireland: "Tell me with whom you are going and I will tell
          you what you are doing."
Cape Verde Islands: "Every week has its Friday."

I love proverbs. As a journalist, I can appreciate the depth of ingenuity and wisdom proverbs offer. They are observations that can help guide our understanding about this world we live in. They provide instruction and even truth. Many cultures use proverbs to deliver valuable knowledge when it comes to everyday experiences.

For example, think about the well-known American proverb "You can't judge a book by its cover." We have all heard this one, yet so many of us don't practice it. Most people do just the opposite through stereotyping and profiling. Unfortunately, I'm sometimes just as guilty as anyone else, and I know better.

Recently, I was pulling my suitcase through the Atlanta airport when I heard a deep, sexy voice behind me say "Hey beautiful." Of course it brought a silly grin to my face. It feels good to be appreciated by the opposite sex. I stopped and turned around to see a tall, mocha-colored man with a bald-head, and a sexy salt and pepper beard, not bad, not bad at all. Then, my eyes swept downward and noticed that he was wearing an Atlanta Braves hoodie over large baggy jeans that hung off of his behind in the typical thug/prison fashion.

I took a deep breath. "What am I supposed to do with that?" This was a grown-ass man. He had to be, at least, forty-something and he was standing in the Atlanta airport with his underwear hanging out. It was impossible not to let my disappointment show.

"Thank you," I said quickly and just kept it moving. Maybe he was a good guy. Maybe he was somebody I could have created a life with. I can't stand to see these young boys with their pants hanging off their butts, so a grown man in that same style was a serious turn off. I don't care what's inside.

A popular Chinese proverb, "Rotten wood cannot be carved," needs to be taken seriously by women today. Especially those who take a guy with some potential and try to shape him into the man they've been looking for. We know it doesn't work like that, but we do it anyway.

Iyanla Vanzant in her book *In the Meantime* attacked the notion of "potential." She said "potential" is a woman's enemy and warned us about it. She explained that "potential" doesn't mean it will definitely happen. And, as we get older "potential" becomes even more problematic when it comes to finding a good mate. If the man has not done whatever it was he was planning to do or needed to do by his fortieth or fiftieth birthday "potential" is questionable.

In other words, what can you do with a fifty-year-old man who is driving a brand-new BMW, but living in his mother's basement? And, what is a man supposed to do with a fifty-year-old woman who owns thousands of dollars worth of name brand purses and shoes, but she is still renting?

Another proverb I find interesting says "Quarrels end, but words once spoken never die." This African proverb suggests that we all need to watch our tongues. The story that comes to mind involves an interracial couple that had been together for more than fifteen years. One day they had a terrible argument, and in a rage, the white husband called his black wife a "stupid, nigger, bitch."

Now, this is a fear that many black men and women have when it comes to interracial relationships. "Stupid" and "bitch" are bad enough, but for a white person to call a black person a "nigger" is unforgivable. They had been together for fifteen years, so that word had to be rattling around inside his head all that time. They stayed together for a while after the incident, but eventually split.

In Ireland people say, "Tell me with whom you are going and I'll tell you what you are doing." This proverb makes me think about those young women who are excited by the bad boy. They know that he's wrong for them, but refuse to do better. Usually, they meet him at a popular club and take him home, then months later they are upset because he is still hanging out at that same club. Duh?

The popularity of the bad boy is a product of the media. Women are shown stereotypes of good guys as nerds and goofballs, while the bad boys are cool and sexy. These images are repetitive and intertextual, which means they are shown over and over again, and we see them everywhere. Eventually, that problematic idea is accepted by society and it impacts how we seek out partners and form relationships.

"It is better to bend than to break," this is a popular proverb attributed to Spain, Italy, Scotland, and Germany in different forms. I connect it to the importance of compromising in relationships, something I have a hard time doing. Of course, there are times when you need to take a stand, but not every time. People need to pick their battles. You can't fight over everything. If you are stubborn, selfish, and insensitive, it will not get you very far, because eventually your significant other will get tired of being bullied. Just like flowers bend toward the warmth of the sun people tend to lean toward the warmth of the heart, especially when that warmth comes from someone they love.

In places like Tanzania, Kenya, Mozambique, and the Congo they say, "If you throw away the fish you could regret it when someone else picks it up." This means that you should appreciate what you have. A good friend tells the story of a long distance relationship she was in where the guy bragged for several months on the phone about what he had and how good he was in bed. When they finally got together, she said she was expecting a Big Mac, but instead, she got a Happy Meal. Rather than getting upset she just enjoyed it!

I was invited in the mid 1990s to write a short story for an erotica anthology. I believe I'm a good writer so how hard could erotica be? I sat down and thought about a subject that was relevant to the time and wrote a piece called "Something Special." I was very happy with this short story. I polished it up and sent it in. Weeks later I received a rejection letter. Apparently, my writing was more sensual than sexual.

Not long after I received the rejection, I saw a call for short stories from another anthology titled *Proverbs for the People*. I searched through various proverb books and websites until I found a perfect match. The theme of my story was a ritual that the main character performed every Friday night. The proverb from the Cape Verde islands was "Every week has its Friday." I submitted the story, it was accepted, and published.

Finally, in her 2013 book, comedian Niecy Nash reminds us that people don't argue when they're naked. That's a good way to think about the Chinese proverb "A man who argues with his wife all day gets no peace/piece at night."

Proverbs are based on common themes, beliefs, values, and norms. They can be used to better understand certain situations and various cultures. Although each of us experiences our own unique journey through life, the path will ultimately be shaped by the world around us.

~~~~~~

Cruisin'

My first cruise took me to the ports of Roatan, Honduras; Belize City, Belize; Puerto Costa Maya and Cozumel, Mexico. After visiting these ports, I remember sitting in my cabin on the way back home watching the rough water outside my window. It really makes you appreciate the life you have when you see how people in other countries struggle for basic survival.

I took a moment to thank God for my success. He made sure that my dreams came true. This cruise wasn't the first time I thought about my success and thanked God for his blessings. I try to thank Him for something every day, and periodically I sit down to make a list of my blessings in order to remind myself that life is good.

When things aren't going exactly the way we want, my brother and I sometimes complain. In one conversation a few years ago, he made a statement that startled me. He said he didn't believe that he was a success.

My brother is a black man with a Master of Fine Arts degree in film, and a retired, tenured professor from a prominent university. He has worked on many award-winning independent films and documentaries, plus we have co-authored two books about black film together. Needless to say, I was surprised that he would question his accomplishments.

There are two areas of success: fantasy and reality. The notion of fantasy success versus reality success has been discussed when it comes to a number of areas including sports, finances, politics, occupations, video games, and even the American dream.

Fantasy success involves those accomplishments that fulfill your wildest dreams. Reality success represents those more normal and common goals that are possible, and even likely to happen. According to Luvvie Ajayi in her 2017 *Ted Talk*, fear is the key to success. When fear is involved, she encourages people to "do it anyway" because in her words "If you want success, fantasy or reality, you should get comfortable with being uncomfortable."

My brother's fantasy success was to be a well-recognized and respected filmmaker like Spike Lee, Tyler Perry or Steven Spielberg. Despite the fact that he is a very talented film director and an excellent editor, he could not find the opening that he needed to break into the industry. Unfortunately, the magnitude of not achieving his fantasy success means that he can not enjoy the reality success he has accomplished.

It is sometimes hard to separate reality success from fantasy success. As a matter of fact, my brother probably didn't see his film ambition as a fantasy at all. We are told from the time we can dream to reach for the stars. So, that's what he did. I've often wondered if we hurt our children by spending so much time pushing them to be better, to be more, rather than allowing them to enjoy who and where they are.

This is not to suggest that my brother couldn't have made it big in film. He definitely has the talent to take a little bit of nothing and make it into something marvelous. But without the connections and opportunities it was tough. After completing his M.F.A., he stayed in Los Angeles for several years trying to find his spot, but it didn't happen. I believe that maybe his pride got in the way. Film is an area where you have to be ready to grovel and beg. This is something my brother doesn't do very well.

Being a published and recognized author I should probably

call my success fantasy because I didn't plan to write novels or non-fiction books. Growing up, I've always loved to read. I admired those authors who could craft a good story like Paule Marshall, Toni Morrison, Zora Neale Hurston, and Walter Mosely, but I didn't think I would ever be one of them. The fact that my fantasy success came true still amazes me and I'm grateful.

My reality success is the place where I look for fulfillment. I wanted to teach at a university, I wanted a family, and I wanted to live a comfortable, happy life. I've accomplished most of my goals. I'm a tenured, associate professor at a research one institution. My daughter has graduated high school and is exploring her future possibilities. I'm living in my dream home with an endless pool.

I've done almost everything I wanted to do except get married. And, as I explained in the first chapter that was my motivation for writing this book. I realize now that marriage just wasn't important enough on my things to do list. I chose career over relationship every time there was a conflict because it was easier to thrive in territory I had control over.

I'm not sure there is anything that I would do differently if I could go back. I accept that my reality is where I am rather than where I thought I would be. I sat and watched the choppy waters outside my window, knowing that without the wind and rain a calm ocean would have less value. When we experience tough times, we can better appreciate the good. Reality is different from fantasy. It is up to each of us to determine how we deal with that difference.

It is our focus that dictates our success, especially in those tough times. I know it's not easy, but I try to focus on the positive as much as possible. For example, the worst experience of my life was losing my baby sister to cancer when she was nineteen-years-old. In the middle of my grief, I looked for something positive. When the doctors told us that she was going to die and there was nothing we could do, I had to find something to hold on to. It was one simple idea that pulled me through "If it's not life or death, it's not a problem."

Since then I have lived by that motto, and it has served me well. It keeps me grounded. When bad things happen, I stop and think: Is this life or death? When the problem is money, I can get more money. When the problem involves a person, I can work with, around or separate from that person. I can focus on what's really important.

Several of the people in my group had cruised before, so they were constantly complaining that they could feel the boat as it rocked back and forth in the water. Apparently, it was a smaller cruise ship, so it didn't have the same buoyancy as the larger ones. This was my first seven-day cruise, so I decided to stay positive. I focused instead on how the ship's rocking back and forth felt kind of nice, especially at night just before sleep came.

~~~~~~

Live Long and Prosper

I consider myself a Trekkie. Although, I don't attend the annual conferences, dress in *Star Trek* fashion, or engage in social media exchanges, I love watching the various television series and movies, including reruns. One reason that I love science fiction is because it helps me think about the future.

For example, what does *Star Trek* tell us about relationships in the future? Captain James T. Kirk, in the original 1966 version sleeps with anything that moves. The 1987 *Next Generation* series features Captain Jean-Luc Picard who pushes love away keeping it at a safe distance. The 1993 *Deep Space Nine* series introduces us to Captain Benjamin Sisko, the first black captain of a space station. He begins as a widowed, single father who eventually falls in love, and marries an independent black woman who is captain of her own ship. The first female *Star Trek* captain Kathryn Janeway leaves her fiancé back on Earth in 1995 in *Star Trek Voyager*. And in 2001, Captain Jonathan Archer's first and only love is the *Starship Enterprise*. These shows represent a variety of possibilities when it comes to relationships in the future.

Science fiction can also help society make important changes. In a 2014 *Yahoo Entertainment* article, Whoopi Goldberg explained that she became a Trekkie because it was the first science fiction television show to include an African American woman in a prominent role. That role was Lt. Uhura as the communications officer.

Lt. Uhura's role in the 1960's was a significant one not only for African American women, but all women. As communications officer on the first Star Trek Enterprise, her character showed that black people could exist on a higher level. As a matter of fact, in the 1968 episode "Plato's Stepchildren" Lt. Uhura shared the first interracial kiss with Captain Kirk. In the documentary, *Pioneers of Television* (2011), Nichelle Nichols, who played the role of Lt. Uhura, tells a story about how she met with Dr. Martin Luther King Jr. when she wanted to quit the show. Dr. King recognized the power of her role in promoting racial equality during the Civil Rights Movement. He encouraged her to stay and she did.

In that same *Yahoo* article, Whoopi said she eventually met with Gene Roddenberry and Rick Berman to ask if she could be added to the cast of characters. She became Guinan a wise and mystical being in *Star Trek: Next Generation*.

Science fiction has some interesting things to say about how women and men's roles are changing. In one episode of *Star Trek: The Next Generation,* First Officer William T. Riker ends up on a planet where women are in control on one side, while a band of men with wives exists on the other side. The women's group is trying to destroy the men's group because they are afraid it will damage their female controlled alternative societal structure. In the end, a decision is made by the leader of the women's group to allow the couples to exist even though she knows it may mean the end of life, as they know it.

Jadzia Dax is the host of a Trill symbiont in *Deep Space Nine*. Symbionts have no gender. Their hosts can be male or female. They live for many years by being implanted into different host bodies. The host lives his or her own life, but also maintains all of the memories from the previous symbionts. Dax is a young, beautiful female and the previous host was an older, male warrior. The opportunity to use a female body for the exploration of male attitudes and behaviors is unique. Plus, her capability to identify with both male and female roles nicely moves her character away from male/female stereotypes.

There is an episode of *Star Trek: Voyager* in which a pregnant woman goes into labor and the hologram doctor is insisting that she push. The woman is screaming from the pain until suddenly the baby goes into distress. The doctor rushes over to a panel and presses a few buttons transporting the baby from the mother's womb into an incubator. I remember laughing out loud. If the baby could be transported in birth removing the horrific pain women have to endure I think they should definitely have that option.

Science fiction is informative when it comes to issues of equality as well. Movies and television shows have given us many strong, powerful women who can do pretty much anything a man can do. For example, one of my favorite film series is *Aliens*. It consisted of three movies where the main character Ellen Ripley fights nasty aliens and wins. I remember reading that for the main character they were supposed to cast a man, but Ridley Scott decided to hire Sigourney Weaver instead. Smart move.

In the *Aliens vs. Predators* movie, I was pleasantly surprised when Alexa Woods, played by Sanaa Lathan, became the only human survivor from the ensemble cast. For the lone survivor to be black and a woman is unusual. There is a running joke in the black community that the black person in most horror and science fiction movies is always the first to die.

There are many other science fiction movies and television shows where women are powerful and respected characters. For example, in *Hunger Games* Jennifer Lawrence as Katniss leads the rebellion against a corrupt government. Samari sword wielding Danai Gurira plays Michonne in *The Walking Dead* television series about zombie survivors. Plus, a fun new series on the SyFy Channel called *Wynonna Earp* is about the female heir of the famed Wyatt Earp. She is following in her great, great grandfather's footsteps killing demons with his long-barrel, Colt Buntline Special named Peacemaker.

In the 2009 reboot of the *Star Trek* movie series; I was disappointed to see that the storyline still fit within a traditional patriarchal structure. Although there are men, women, and aliens working together on the bridge, shared social expectations from the past concerning men and women suggest that males should protect females and females should look for help. As a matter of fact, Melissa Silverstein in the *Huffington Post* complained that there were stereotypes tied to all three major female characters. Two were depicted as mothers, and one was a girlfriend.

Star Trek Into Darkness, the sequel, changes the stereotype just a little by bringing in Dr. Carol Marcus who helps stop her father's evil plans. Finally, there is a major change in the third movie of the series, *Star Trek Beyond* (2016). Lt. Uhura is no longer Spock's girlfriend. She joins the fighting along with a new female alien warrior named Jaylah.

When thinking about changing gender attitudes, roles, and identities in the 21st-century sociology research can offer some interesting notions. First, being feminine or masculine is not seen in the same way as it was in the 19th and 20th centuries.

For example, biological issues are pertinent when it comes to thinking about future gender roles and equality. Today, we can no longer argue that men perpetuate an energy that is considered masculine, while women have a softer, feminine energy. Not everybody fits the norm. There are some men who think and function with a more feminine nature, and some women who think and act more masculine.

Under the stereotypical societal norm, a feminine nature makes the person a wimp, a crybaby, and other negative terms. They care too much. They give in too easily. They are drama oriented. As a result, they frequently get taken advantage of, mistreated, used, and sometimes abused. Over the years, women have had to force themselves to be more selfish, get tougher, and work hard to eliminate this stereotype.

Second, science fiction themes are often lifted from reality. For instance, America is fast becoming a country of haves and have-nots with the have-nots consisting mainly of women and children. It doesn't make sense that women still make less than men even when doing the same job, and black women make less than men, and white women. There are many science fiction movies that explore inequality in our society now and in the future. Examples include *Elysium* (2013), *Avatar* (2009), *District 9* (2009), *In Time* (2011), and *Hunger Games* (2012, 2013, 2014, 2015).

In the Star Trek universe the importance of money is minimized. Everyone has what he or she needs for basic comfort. The one culture that portrays capitalistic greed is the Ferengi. They can be found in *Star Trek: Deep Space Nine, Star Trek: Voyager,* and *Star Trek: Discovery.* The Ferengi culture is obsessed with money, focusing on profit and trade, often cheating and scamming. Women in the Ferengi society don't wear clothes, they don't argue with their husbands, and they don't go out in public. Even the Ferengi religion perpetuates the principles of capitalism as they focus on wealth getting them into the divine treasury when they die rather than going to the vault of eternal destitution.

The Ferengi could be compared to the powerful one percent in today's society. They are reaping most of the rewards from our economy. A 2018 article in *The Guardian* reported that the richest people in the world will own two-thirds of all wealth by 2030. While the National Center for Children in Poverty reports that forty-three percent of children live in low-income families, and persistent poverty is the single greatest threat to a child's well-being (2018).

Speaking of power, in a few movies and television shows women have been cast as president of the United States. *Independence Day: Resurgence* (2016) featured Sela Ward as POTUS. Television shows like *Veep* with Julia Louis-Dreyfus, Alfre Woodard in *State of Affairs*, Bellamy Young in *Scandal,* and *24's* Cheryl Jones have also made the presidential leap. A female American president is relevant in science fiction because, when we had the chance to elect our first real female president we failed. She was one of the most qualified candidates to ever run for that office, and definitely more qualified than the man who won. I actually heard women say that they couldn't or wouldn't vote for a female president. They didn't believe a woman should lead this country.

As women we have been taught that our social role is dependent on men. We are stereotyped as inferior and weak. We struggle to find our place, but ultimately many of us buy into the problematic attitudes of patriarchy. What happens to people who continue to do the same thing over and over expecting different results?

Images and messages in science fiction can help us think about the changes we need to make in this society. If we allow gender roles and stereotypes to persist, it will be hard to move forward. Women are fighting in the military beside men. Women are working in male oriented jobs like construction and engineering. Women are becoming pastors and bishops in various religions. Women are more involved in politics, computer science, business, and finance. We are proving that we can literally do anything.

Women's roles in this world must change because with age and experience women are changing. It makes sense that gender attitudes, images, and identities have transformed. When I look at who I am now versus who I was twenty or thirty years ago, there is a huge difference. When I imagine twenty or thirty years from now, I'm sure there will be even more changes for my daughter and her generation to embrace.

The future is also portrayed through alien races in science fiction. There are interesting examples of life in the future not necessarily based on earth. The Vulcans are my favorite alien race with their copper-based blood and pointed ears. What I like most is the ability they have to maintain complete control of their feelings and emotions. I think that would be an awesome skill. In an episode from the *Star Trek: Enterprise* series, T'Pol's Vulcan character allows herself to experience human love. With that love comes uncertainty, pain, and suffering, so she decides it is better to let go of her emotions and stay in control.

The Klingons are depicted as a violent race, so Worf's version of love is aggressive and animalistic. This fits the stereotype of African American men, and Worf's brown skin makes him obviously different. He is played by an African American male actor named Michael Dorn. In one episode, as part of the relationship between Worf and a Klingon woman they growled at each other and positioned themselves more like they were about to do battle than make love. In another episode, Worf explained to Guinan that he couldn't have a relationship with a non-Klingon female because she would be too fragile.

A final interesting notion to think about in science fiction is what happens if we move outside of humanity. How might artificial intelligence influence our changing society? Imagine an android that you could program to do whatever you need him to do. Data, the android in *Star Trek: Next Generation,* was designed with all of the correct parts he needed to please a woman.

Think about it. We could literally place our order on Amazon: height, weight, personality, looks, and abilities. Maybe even get free delivery! Like former talk show host Arsenio Hall, I would put this in the category of things that make you go hummmmmmmmmmm.

~~~~~~

God is love

A friend once asked me "If God is love where is He in the world today?" It's a good question when we look at what's going on: continuous wars in the Middle East, police in America murdering young, unarmed black men, terrorist groups kidnapping African girls, and white supremacists marching against progress in America. The only answer I could give her was that God gave human beings free will and many are using it incorrectly.

I believe as a Christian that "God is love." This declaration can be found in The New Testament 1 John 4:8. I believe we were created by God to love. I believe that God's love is unconditional. However, we live in a world today that has moved love away from God, far away from the divine.

When it comes to love today, we might as well toss coins in a fountain or chant, "he loves me, he loves me not" while throwing petals from a flower up into the air. So much of the love in this world is not connected to God. It's secular and profane. It's deceitful and ugly. It's fleeting and distant. It's painful and unsatisfying.

A former student introduced me to a book by psychologist Bruno Bettelheim called *The Uses of Enchantment: The Meaning and Importance of Fairy Tales* (1976). Bettelheim argued that the separation of Adam and Eve from the Garden of Eden sparked an intense need for love that remains inside each of us, as we are all descendants of Adam and Eve.

This is an interesting idea because it means, theoretically, that we all find ourselves in a search for not just any love, but God's love, the love that Adam and Eve lost. And maybe that's the real problem. We watch hundreds of movies and listen to thousands of songs about love, but nothing measures up to the real love, the divine love that we lost.

We are so confused about love and values today that the movie *Pretty Woman* can be seen on the *Family Channel*. This is the story of a prostitute who meets a rich man while standing out on the street corner. The totally ridiculous plot suggests that in one week the prostitute miraculously changes the rich man's life. So, he rescues her with a marriage proposal and makes all of her dreams come true. A movie that makes prostitution acceptable is not really a movie that perpetuates family values.

My friend Alyssa calls this storyline the adventures of Captain-Save-A-Ho. She says there are men out there looking for women that need to be rescued. Apparently, it has something to do with power, ego, and maybe even control.

Captain-Save-A-Ho is real. I've heard stories about these men (of course the names have usually been changed). For example, a woman named Tammy was an alcoholic who didn't finish high school. She had two kids by two different men, and she was rescued by an electrical engineer named Daniel. They are living a very comfortable life in North Carolina.

Shantay was working as a waitress at Hooters, flaunting her ghettofabulous flair when she met her politically active husband. Late one night while waiting on his table they connected. After the marriage, he went on to become a prominent politician in Texas.

Of course, many of us know the story of that woman in college who was not a serious football fan. However, she attended every game and slept with a third of the team. Ultimately, when his name was called in the fourth round of the NFL draft, he went pro, and she went with him.

Career oriented, independent women don't need to be rescued, at least not like that. Therefore, Captain-Save-A-Ho is usually not looking for us. But, just because we're not struggling that doesn't mean we wouldn't mind a little help. Yes, we're college professors, attorneys, public relations executives, business owners, ministers, computer techs, television producers, politicians, and in hundreds of other prominent professions, but we still yearn for the love and support of a good man.

Sarah Jessica Parker as Carrie Bradshaw in an episode of *Sex and the City* examined this question. Charlotte questioned whether or not all women really just want to be rescued. Carrie tells her that women their age are not supposed to think that way let alone say it out loud. Charlotte replies: "I'm sorry, but it's true. I've been dating since I was fifteen. I'm exhausted. Where is he?"

During the show, Parker discovers that even though some independent women don't want to admit it most believe that life would better if they had someone to share the burdens, as well as the good times with. So, her conclusion at the end of the episode was, "Yeah, on some level all women want to be rescued."

I've never been a needy woman. I don't need a man to mow the yard, empty the trash or service the car. If I can't do something myself, I can hire somebody to do it. I don't need to be rescued, but it would be nice to have somebody in my life to do those things for me, somebody to share the daily ups and downs, somebody to build a meaningful and secure future with.

A gay friend once told me that his baby sister was constantly in and out of relationships. One day he heard his mother say: "Your brother has held on to his man for more that twenty years. What's your problem?"

That's a very good question, what is our problem?

Maybe our problem is too many hopes and dreams that are wrapped around the fairy tale idea of love. We immerse ourselves in reoccurring fantasies. We search for love like a detective searches for clues. But when we open our hearts and love fails we are forced to retreat. We build a fence to protect our heart, and that works about as good as the more than six hundred miles of fence already built along the Mexico-United States border. Just like illegal immigrants still find their way into the U.S., insincere, trifling, and undeserving men slip past our perimeters to hurt us again. I thought, as I got older I would get better at spotting the losers, playas, and tricksters. Apparently, the losers, playas, and tricksters are also improving their game.

Maybe we are not looking for the right kind of men. Maybe we need to accept basic, honest, hard-working men even if they are below our status. Maybe we are looking in the wrong places. Maybe we should give up on nightclubs, online dating sites, casinos, and even AA meetings. Maybe our attitude is the problem. Maybe we talk too much, we're inconsistent, argumentative, and judgmental, we have too much pride, and we don't know how to let go of past baggage. These comments are just a few that I've heard over the years concerning black women and love.

I wish I had the answer. I could bottle or box it and get rich. I don't have the answer, but I do want to suggest that we start with a simple concept "God is love." Then, follow that with the two primary commandments concerning love: put God first, loving Him with all of our heart, soul, and mind, and love our neighbors as ourselves.

I believe that these two commandments can move us closer to divine love; the kind of love that we have been searching for since Adam and Eve messed up, the kind of love we really want.

~~~~~~~

Letting Go

This is another hard one. When it is something I really want I have a problem letting go. Dreams are said to be one way that our subconscious helps us think through the problems in our lives. I can be struggling with something all day, and in a dream the solution comes.

For example, I remember clearly a dream I had after a bad break up. In the dream, I was living in an apartment building, but it was not someplace that I recognized. It was one of those buildings that had businesses on the lower floors and apartments or condos up top. In reality, I've never lived in one of those.

Anyway, I was rushing through the place getting dressed to go out, and several suitors knocked on the door interrupting me. The first knock was someone from my past who wanted me back. Actually, he was somebody I wouldn't mind getting back with. The second knock came from someone I didn't know. As somebody new, he reminded me about the unknown possibilities that were still out there. When the third knock came, I looked out the peephole, and didn't bother to open the door. He showed up to confirm the fact that I needed to keep looking.

The dream shifted, and I was at a football game sitting in the bleachers with a female friend cheering on one of the teams. A non-descript man approached me. He was very arrogant and not the type of guy I would be interested in. I had my eye on someone who was not paying me any attention. He was surrounded by several girls flaunting their long weaves, thin bodies, and phony smiles.

Suddenly, I reached up to scratch my head and realized that I still had curlers in my hair. I screamed. I was all dressed up and thinking I was looking good with curlers all over my head. I yanked the curlers out while fussing at my friend because she didn't bother to tell me.

My friend allowed me to get it all out, then said to me very calmly: "If he doesn't want you because you have curlers in your hair then he's not the one."

I knew that was the answer as soon as I woke up. I had blamed my broken relationship on me. Of course, it was something I did wrong. I worried about the extra fifty pounds I'm carrying because it means I don't fit into society's idea of beauty. I complain because my life is not simple. I'm a perfectionist who is not perfect, and my doubts never go away.

As I thought about that dream, I could replace the curlers with anything: weight, career, attitude, success, whatever, and the answer would still be the same. This is who I am. If he doesn't want me based on who I am, he's not the one for me. And, taking it a step further, it is his loss.

"So how do you know if he's the right one?" A young friend asked me this question on the telephone one night. She couldn't see me shrug my shoulders before I responded.

"I'm fifty-years-old and I don't have the answer," I told her.

She continued: "I wonder about those people who say it was love at first sight. Do you think there's such a thing as love at first sight?"

I took a deep breath. "Just because we haven't found it doesn't mean it's not out there."

My friend spent many years waiting on the man she loved to marry her. They had a child together when they were young and he basically performed the role of husband and father. They didn't live together, but he cleaned her car and made sure it was running well. He mowed the yard. They went to movies, dinner, and other events together. However, he made it clear that he was not interested in marriage.

More than anything my friend wanted to get married. When she finally woke up, she woke up with a vengeance.

"I will never again make a man my priority while he keeps me as an option," she vowed.

She started to date and met a couple of good guys, but still no marriage. One day, as we both complained about men and relationships, she asked: "What if we're exactly where we're supposed to be at this moment?"

Her question stopped my tirade cold. It was a very good question. What if I was exactly where I was supposed to be? Could I have lived my life the way I wanted to live it with a man attached? I know there are successful women who juggle family and career, but maybe that's not me.

In his book, *Blue Like Jazz* Donald Miller suggests that love is something you must choose. If I'm honest, love was not the choice I made. Our choices create our future. So, I have to accept the fact that my choices concerning love and career have brought me to exactly where I am today.

One of my favorite movies is an old 1992 classic *Boomerang* with Eddie Murphy and Robin Givens. It is one of my favorites because it explores how our choices make us who we are, and ultimately bring us what we want. Marcus, Eddie Murphy's character is a playa. Once the chase is over it is time to move on. Robin Givens is a female version of Marcus and he gets played. Halle Berry is Angela a love interest. In the movie, Angela tells Marcus that love is more than something you just fall into. She says that falling in love is not enough. Once you fall in love you must choose to stay there. That's really the answer isn't it?

I was in love with my high school sweetheart. He was tall, milk chocolate, and fine. We could have gotten married, had kids, and lived a pretty good life, but I made a different choice. I was in love with my college boyfriend. We got engaged and talked seriously about a future together. I loved him. I thought I would grow old with him until I made a different choice. I hoped that my baby's daddy was the man that I could fulfill my dreams with. But he wasn't, and we separated. I made a different choice.

~~~~~~

A Life Worth Living

It was around two o'clock in the morning. I had just finished a paper for an ethnomusicology class. I hit the print button, and then went into the kitchen to get myself a glass of water. When the paper finished printing, I stapled it together. Since my computer sat on the dining room table in my apartment, I had to walk over to the living room couch to slip the paper into my briefcase.

The living room was dark, except for a light shining from the dining room that cast shadows across the floor. When I suddenly felt a bump followed by a sharp stinging sensation on my big toe I screamed and kicked my right leg forward. The kick forced whatever it was to let go. It slammed up against the wall and was stunned long enough for me to run into the kitchen, grab a glass bowl, and cover it. That night seems surreal now, but when I flipped on the living room light, there was a scorpion under that bowl. I did not think I would live through the night.

I panicked and called my next-door neighbor who was also one of my best friends. I could hear her stumbling down the stairs on the other side of the wall between our townhouses. After opening the front door for her, I pointed to the bowl. She called poison control while I ran upstairs to put on some clothes so she could take me to the hospital.

The lady at the poison control center didn't think it was a big deal. She asked about my weight and the size of the scorpion, then told my neighbor there would be some swelling and pain for a few days, but I should be fine.

Moving from the Midwest to Texas, everything I'd ever heard about scorpions was connected to death. Apparently, the amount of venom in this scorpion could have been deadly to my dog or a small child. Before the lady hung up, she warned us to be careful because scorpions usually traveled in pairs. Needless to say, I didn't sleep at all that night. I was worried that if I closed my eyes they wouldn't open again. I called an exterminator first thing in the morning, and he came right over to clear out the townhouse.

Many of us have heard that saying: "Someday your life will flash before your eyes, make sure it is a life worth watching." That night I promised God that if he got me through I would not waste whatever time I had left. I wanted my life to be worth watching. And I've tried to keep that promise.

An interesting article in *Psychology Today* suggested that those things that add meaning to your life or the stuff that makes you happy are key to a life worth living. He offers two areas to consider, work and play.

I could handle work. That's what I did best. After completing my Ph.D., I interviewed for both teaching and administrative positions over a two-year period at universities across the country from San Jose State to Georgia Southern.

At every interview, someone would say, "We'd love to hire one (a minority Ph.D.) but they're not out there."

And I would question them, "How many do you have in your Ph.D. program?"

The answer would come back, "None, maybe one, every now and then two."

"So, where do you expect them to come from if you're not making them?" I asked.

According to an August 2017 report from the American Academy of Arts and Sciences, the numbers aren't much better thirty years later concerning African Americans or other minorities in graduate programs. In 2015, doctorates completed by underrepresented, domestic minorities in humanities was a little over ten percent, and for master and professional degrees, it was about fifteen percent.

I often shake my head when I hear people talk about how much Affirmative Action did for minorities. Don't get me wrong, it helped a little, but the group that received the most benefits from Affirmative Action was white women. In that same 2015 study, there is a stark difference as women earned sixty-one percent of master and professional degrees, and fifty-four percent of doctoral degrees.

I remember telling my mom I wish I could clone myself and she said: "You can."

She was right. I could make sure more minorities get into Ph.D. programs and graduate. So, at my University of Iowa interview I explained what I wanted to do. I told the faculty that I planned to help more domestic minority candidates get admitted and graduate with advances degrees. They agreed to support my goal. Coming back to Iowa was the last thing I had planned to do, but I came back with a purpose. At Iowa my path became clear.

On tenure track I needed to publish. Iowa is a research one institution with a reduced teaching load allowing faculty to conduct research and write. Publishing was not something I was doing before, so I had to figure some things out. I started working on several journal articles and book chapters until I got the opportunity to finish a novel that I started in graduate school.

This was the early nineties when Terry McMillan forced the publishing doors open for many African American authors. I revised a novel manuscript and sent it to an interested agent, but she said it wasn't ready. A friend and former newspaper reporter edited the manuscript, I made the changes she suggested and sent it back. Again the agent wasn't happy. What was most frustrating was that the agent couldn't tell me what exactly was wrong. It felt like I was wasting time, so I tossed the manuscript up into my closet and went back to my academic research.

God stepped in. I had started a walking regimen four evenings a week. I had been faithful for probably about four months. Early one Friday morning, I was suddenly wide awake with a voice telling me to get up and go walk. I had never walked in the morning, but if I didn't do it then, I would not get my four days in because I was going out of town that afternoon. I tried to ignore the voice for a while, but finally got up and stomped over to the recreation center.

With my headphones on, I walked around the track listening to one of my favorite artists Al Jarreau. There was only one other person on the track, an older man walking behind me. He soon caught up and said something. I tried not to show how irritated I was. I am not a morning person, and I honestly don't like morning people. I just wanted to finish my walk in peace. I took a deep breath then removed my headphones.

"Does this stuff really work?" He asked jokingly.

"They say it does, so I'm giving it a try," I quickly replied. I was about to replace my headphones, but he kept talking. To be honest, I don't know what the man said during the first couple of minutes because I was fussing in my head rather than listening. Finally, I heard the word "writer" and my mind shifted. He was explaining that he had graduated from the esteemed Iowa Writers Workshop and currently had five published novels.

"I know God sent you to me," he said.

I stopped walking.

This man was finishing his sixth novel where the main character was a young, African American doctor. He was looking for an African American to read the manuscript over to make sure that the dialogue and description didn't sound like it was written by an older, white, Jewish man.

I told him about the draft of my novel that the agent said wasn't ready, but she couldn't tell me what to do with it, and we agreed to exchange manuscripts that afternoon before I left town.

His book *The Black Samaritan* was published soon after and my agent sold my first novel *So Good, An African American Love Story* a few months later. I had never walked in the morning before that day, and I have never walked in the morning since.

When I think about a life worth living my own success has been wonderful, but my real satisfaction comes from working in education. A young undergraduate who was smoking pot and messing up in class when we met turned it around and ultimately became an attorney. A young cousin that I took under my wings was told by an uncle that she wasn't going to be anybody special. She proved him wrong. Not only did she earn a bachelor's degree, she went on to get her masters in computer science. I counseled a college athlete who was not happy with the sports program at Iowa. He eventually decided to quit even though it meant losing his scholarship. Not only did he finish his undergraduate degree, but he also went on to earn a masters degree, and plans to get a Ph.D. in African American Studies.

My goal has been realized with many undergraduate and graduate students. I have had the honor of working with black, Latino, Asian, Caucasian, and mixed graduate students. I help them through their programs as an advisor or as a member of the committee. I was especially proud to hood my first African American Ph.D. advisee. She was in the journlism graduate program before I arrived and was struggling. Many of the faculty in the department didn't believe she could do it. I agreed to co-chair her committee with another faculty member. She walked across the stage to receive her degree in 1995.

It took me a while to acknowledge that the Lord had a plan for my life. And seeing his plan come together has been truly miraculous. In 2001, I accepted the Interim Director position at the School of Journalism for one year. We were in the process of planning and fundraising for a new journalism building. I met regularly with the architects concerning the building design and worked with foundation representatives on fundraising efforts.

This was excellent preparation a few years later when members of Bethel A.M.E. Church in Iowa City decided to expand the sanctuary. Bethel was a tiny, historical, African Methodist Episcopal church built in 1868. We were a small congregation of about thirty adults with a great pastor, and very few resources. As co-chair of the fundraising campaign committee, I called the architect from my Journalism School experience, and he agreed to help. He introduced us to a wonderful contractor who also provided extensive support. Plus, the UI foundation representative that I had forged a friendship with conducted a fundraising workshop for interested church members.

At the same time that we hustled to raise the down payment for a mortgage, we also had to fulfill various city regulations and requirements from the Historical Society. For example, the city told us we had to buy the property next door based on the size of the new building. We didn't have the money, but we continued to have faith. Despite the fact that the house next door was not for sale, the owner sold it to us. After we raised the down payment for the new building, four out of five banks turned us down for a mortgage. The fifth bank, a local bank, supported our vision. On Sunday, August 1, 2010, we moved into the new Bethel A.M.E. sanctuary and fellowship hall. God is Good!

Every morning I try to remember that new opportunities are out there. I've accepted the responsibility and the consequences for each choice I made. I've found a way to be thankful for the good and bad because all of it has shaped my journey.

This was not an easy book to write. With fiction I can make it up, but in each of these essays I had to examine the fragments of real experience. My life has been sometimes exciting, sometimes discouraging, sometimes motivating, sometimes painful, and sometimes liberating. But, has my life been a life worth living? Absolutely!

The End

~~~~~~

Works Cited

Baby Boomers

Colby, Sandra and Ortman, Jennifer. "The Baby Boom Cohort in the United States: 2012-2060." *U.S. Census Report,* 2014. https://www.census.gov/prod/2014pubs/p25-1141.

Greenfieldboyce, Nell. "Pageant Protest Sparked Bra Burning Myth." *NPR Morning Edition,* September 5, 2008. https://.www.npr.org/templates/story/story.php?storyId =94240375

"Is 50 the new 30?" *ABC News*. December 31, 2005. http://abc news.go.com/GMA/Health/story?id=1455634.

"King Speaks to March on Washington." *History.com*, August 28, 1963. http://www.history.com/this-day-in-history/king-speaks-to-march-on-washington.

Fifty/Fifty

Waddell, Nick. "Marriage Means Less Chance of Depression for Men, Opposite for Women: Study." *Cantech*, July 24, 2017. https://www.cantechletter.com/2017/07/marriage-means-less-chance-depression-men-opposite-women-study/.

The "L" Word

Alcoholics Anonymous Website. Alcoholics Anonymous Publishing World Services Inc., 1952, 1953, 1981. https://www.aa.org/assets/en_US/smf-121_en.pdf.

Saints and Sinners

The King James Bible. Genesis, 1 Corinthians, Exodus, Judges, and Book of Ruth. BibleGateway Website. 1611.

Knock on Wood

Berry, Venise. *Colored Sugar Water*. New York: Dutton Penguin, 2002.

Hall, Judy. *Sun Signs for Lovers: An Astrological Guide to Love, Sex and Relationships*. London: Octopus Publishing, 2005.

Potter, Carole. *Knock on Wood and Other Superstitions*. New York: Bonanza Books, 1983.

The Book of Job

Haney, Stephanie. "Ladies, Take My Advice: College is Your Best Bet for Finding a Husband." *The Los Angeles Times,* June 2, 2016. http://www.latimes.com/home/la-hm-0604-laaffairs-20160531-snap-story.html#.

Hilmantel, Robin. "Why You Shouldn't Find a Husband in College." *Women's Health,* April 4, 2013.

Wang, Wendy. "Interracial Marriage: Who is Marrying Out?" *PEW Research Center FactTank*. June 12, 2015.

Schafer, Jack. "Broken Heart Syndrome." *Psychology Today,* December 29, 2016. https://www.psychologytoday.com/blog/let-their-words-do-the-talking/201612/broken-heart-syndrome.

"Women and Heart Disease Fact Sheet." *Center for Disease Control*, Atlanta, Georgia, August 23, 2017.

Valentine's Day

Graves, Dan. "Martyrdom of St. Valentine." *Christianity.com,* April 28, 2010. https://www.christianity.com/church/church-history/timeline/1-300/martyrdom-of-st-valentine-11629626.html

Lewis, C.S. *The Four Loves*. New York: Harcourt Brace, 1960.

A Hopeful Romantic

"Marriage in Black America." *Black Demographics*, 2014. http://blackdemographics.com/households/marriage-in-black-america.

Noelle-Neumann, Elizabeth. *The Spiral of Silence: Public Opinion-Our Social Skin.* Chicago: University of Chicago Press, 1993.

Turner, Kathleen. *Romancing the Stone*, 1984. http://www.imdb.com/title/tt0088011/.

Hoochies, Hotties and Hoes

Dukes of Hazzard. Warner Brothers, 2005. http://www.imdb.com/title/tt0377818/.

Schor, Juliet. *Born to Buy: The Commercialized Child and the New Consumer Cult.* New York: Simon and Schuster, 2014.

Late Bloomers

Lee, Spike. *She's Gotta Have it.* New York: 40 Acres & a Mule Filmworks, August 8, 1986. http://www.imdb.com/title/tt0091939/.

What's Love Got to Do With It?

Davies, Madeline. "The Flavor of Love Casting Process is Sad and Fascinating." *Jezebel,* March 6, 2014. https://jezebel.com/the-flavor-of-love-casting-process-is-sad-and-fascinati-1538172555.

Divorce Court. "Celebrity Divorcees Pay High Price:10 highest Divorce Settlements paid by Women in Hollywood." January 22, 2015. https://www.divorcecourt.com/2015/01/22/10-highest-divorce-settlements-paid-by-women-in-hollywood/.

Flavor of Love with Flavor Flav. VH1 TV, 2006-2008. http://www.imdb.com/title/tt0488262/.

Hines, Nickolaus. "The History of the Gold Digger." *All-that-is-interesting.com*, January 12, 2016. http://all-that-is-interesting.com/gold-digger.

Hopwood, Avery. *Gold Diggers*. Performance Archives. Warner Brothers, October 13, 1919. http://www.performingarts archive.com/Broadway/Gold-diggers_1919/Gold-diggers _1919.htm.

Kim, Jen. "Be the Best Gold Digger You Can Be." *Psychology Today*, July 25, 2011. https://www.psychologytoday.com/ blog/valley-girl-brain/201107/be-the-best-gold-digger-you-can-be.

Lewis, Anna and Baxter-Wright, Dusty. "Kim Kardashian and Kanye West: A Timeline of their relationship." *Cosmopolitan Magazine*, January 16, 2018. http://www. cosmopolitan.com/uk/entertainment/news/a47556/kim-kardashian-kanye-west-timeline-relationship/.

Lorre, Rose Maura. "How Flavor of Love Cast Hottie New York and other Memorable Contestants." *Vulture*, March 6, 2014. http://www.vulture.com/2014/03/how-flavor-of-love-found-its-memorable-cast.html.

Marcus, Stephanie. "What You Don't Know About Kim Kardashian's Sex Tape Leak." *HuffPost*, March 28, 2017. https://www.huffingtonpost.com/entry/kim-kardashian-sex-tape-anniversaryus_58daa8dbe4b037bd82caea9f.

Stanger, Patti. *Millionaire Matchmaker*. Bravo TV, January 2008 – March 29, 2015. The Millionaire's Club. http://www. millionairesclub123.com.

Swartz, Mimi. "How to Marry a Millionaire." *Texas Monthly*, October 1994. https://www.texasmonthly.com/articles/ how-to-marry-a-millionaire/.

The PostGame Staff. "NBA Rookies Get Schooled in the Ways of Certain Women." *The PostGame.com*, August 28, 2012. http://www.thepostgame.com/blog/dish/201208/nba-rook ies-get-schooled-ways-women.

Turner, Tina. "What's Love Got to do With It?" *Private Dancer* Album. Capital Records, 1983.

Watkins, Jade. "'I married him for security': Crystal Harris Reveals the Real Reason Why She Married Hugh Heffner." *Daily Mail.com*. February 7, 2013. http://www.dailymail. co.uk/tvshowbiz/article-2275301/I-married-security-Crystal-Harris-reveals-real-reason-married-Hugh-Hefner.

West, Kanye. "Gold Digger." *Late Registration* Roc-A-Fella/Def Jam, 2005. https://www.amazon.com/Gold-Digger-Kanye-West/dp/B000BDIZ94.

From Fact to Fiction

Berry, Venise. *All of Me, A Voluptuous Tale*. New York: Dutton Penguin, 2000.

Fratello, Jenna. "What's Average? Size 16 is the New Normal for U.S. Women." *Today.com*, September 29, 2016. https://www.today.com/style/what-s-average-size-16-new-normal-us-women-t103315.

Narins, Elizabeth. "The 21 Craziest Diets Ever – Debunked." *Cosmopolitan Magazine*. January 21, 2015. http://www.cosmopolitan.com/healthfitness/advice/a35415/craziest-diets-ever-debunked/.

Research on Males and Eating Disorders. *National Eating Disorders Association* (NEDA), 2016. https://www.nationaleatingdisorders.org/research-males-and-eating-disorders.

Janet Jackson - Control

Fazal, Mahmood. "Chemicals They Use to Cut Drugs." *Vice,* October 13, 2017. https://www.vice.com/en_us/article/59d8wd/dealers-describe-the-worst-chemicals-they-use-to-cut-drugs.

Perry, Tyler. *Why Did I Get Married*. Lions Gate Entertainment, 2007. http://www.imdb.com/title/tt0906108/.

Perry, Tyler. *Daddy's Little Girls*. Lions Gate Entertainment, 2007. http://www.imdb.com/title/tt0778661/.

Playin' the Game

Harvey, Steve. *Act Like a Lady, Think Like a Man: What Men Really Think About Love, Relationships, Intimacy and Commitment.* New York: Amistad, 2011.

Angry Black Women

Andrews, Helena. *Bitch is the New Black.* New York: Harper Perennial, 2011.

Ellis, Judith Howard. "Michelle Obama: I'm not 'some angry black woman'." *The Washington Post,* January 11, 2012. https://www.washingtonpost.com/blogs/she-thepeople/post/michelle-obama-im-not-some-angry-black woman/2012/01/11/gIQAmCDMrP_blog.html?utm_term=.6f9662289bea.

Hooks, bell. *Ain't I a Woman? Black Women and Feminism.* New York: Routledge, 2014.

Hughley, D. L. "Tough Words on Politics and Women." *NPR Interview,* 2012. https://www.npr.org/2012/10/25/163628656/d-l-hughley-tough-words-on-politics-and-women.

Hurston, Zora Neale. *Their Eyes Were Watching God.* New York: Harper Perennial Modern Classics, 1937, 2013.

Kerwin, Ann Marie. "The 'Angry Black Woman' Makes Real Women Angry." *Ad Age,* September 27, 2017. http://ad age.com/article/media/angry-black-woman-makes-real-women angry/310633/?utmcampaign= SocialFlow&utm_source=Facebook&utmmedium=Social.

Lee, Malcolm. *The Best Man.* Universal Studios, 1999. http://www.imdb.com/title/tt0168501/.

Loggins, Ameer Hassan. "ESPN's Jemele Hill Being Reduced to an Angry Black Woman." *The Guardian,* October 12, 2017. https://www.theguardian.com/commentisfree/2017/oct/12/espn-jemele-hill-angry-black-woman-suspension-nfl.

Stanley, Alessandra. "Wrought in Rhimes Images: Viola
    Davis Plays Shonda Rhimes's Latest Tough Heroine."*The
    New York Times,* September 18, 2014. https://www.ny
    times.com/2014/09/21/arts/television/viola-davis-plays-
    shonda-rhimess-latest-tough-heroine.html.

Driven

Selleck, Tom. *Blue Bloods*. CBS Television, 2010-2018.
    http://www.cbs.com/shows/blue_bloods/cast/62421/.
Queen. *Another One Bites the Dust*. EMI/Elektra, 1980.

My Baby's Daddy

Gregory, Deborah. "Venise Berry: A Sisterly Novel. People/
    Wordstar." *Essence Magazine,* September 1996, p.78.

Tired Black Men

Alexander, Tim. *Diary of a Tired Black Man*. Atlanta, GA:
    Independent Film, 2008.
Bohdan, Michael. *Cockroach Hall of Fame*. Plano Texas,
    2007-2012. https://www.atlasobscura.com/places/
    cockroach-hall-fame-museum or https://www.youtube.
    com/watch?v=yUpMxz0Fc3chttps:/.
Hustle and Flow. "Three 6 Mafia make Oscar history." It's
    Hard Out Here for a Pimp. *Billboard,* March 3, 2006.
    https://www.billboard.com/articles/news/59507/three-
    6-mafia-ready-to-make-oscar-history.
Oprah. "What I know for Sure." *O Magazine,* 2018. http://
    www.oprah.com/omagazine/what-i-know-for-sure-
    oprah-winfrey.
Parton, Dolly. "Travelin' Thru." *Transamerica,* 2006. http://
    www.imdb.com/title/tt0407265/awards.
Thomas-Lester, Avis. "Oscar Winner Hits Angry Chord." *The
    Washington Post,* March 7, 2006. http://www.washington
    post.com/wpdyn/content/article/2006/03/06/
    AR2006030601461.html.

York, Kathleen and Michael Becker. "In the Deep." *Crash*, 2006. http://www.imdb.com/title/tt0375679/awards.

Peace My Sister
Gray, John. *Men are from Mars Women are from Venus*. New York: Harper Paperbacks, 2012

SweetChocolate
Soul Singles website. Dana Point: CA. https://soulsingles.com.

Black Love in a Big White House
Dennis, David. "Cornell West and Tavis Smiley Do a Disservice to African Americans." *The Guardian*, July 26, 2013. https://www.theguardian.com/commentisfree/2013/jul/26/cornel-west-tavis-smiley/disservice to African Americans/.

Dowd, Maureen. "The Supreme Court: Conservative Black Judge Clarence Thomas is named to Marshall's Court Seat." *The New York Times,* July 2, 1991. http://www.nytimes.com/1991/07/02/us/supreme-court-conservative-black-judge-clarence-thomas-named-marshall-s-court.html?pagewanted=all.

Obama, Barack. *The Audacity of Hope*. New York: Vintage Press, 2008.

Obama, Barack. "Remarks by President on Trayvon Martin." *The White House Archives,* July 19, 2013. https://obamawhitehouse.archives.gov/the-press-office/2013/07/19/remarks-president-trayvon-martin.

Obama, Michelle. "Remarks by the First Lady at a Campaign Event at Morgan State University." *The White House Archives,* September 22, 2012. https://obamawhitehouse.archives.gov/the-pressoffice/2012/09/22/remarks-first-lady-campaign-event-morgan-state-university.

Romano, Andrew. "Barack and Michelle: The Millennials Dream Couple." *Newsweek,* February 13, 2009. http://www.newsweek.com/barack-and-michelle-millennials-dream-couple-82739.

Vassar, Lyndra. "Tavis Smiley and Cornel West Criticize President Obama, Steve Harvey Responds." *Essence,* August 13, 2011. https://www.essencecom/2011/08/13/ tavis-smiley-and-cornel-west-criticize-president-obama-steve-harvey-responds.

My Heavenly Bed

Downing, Keith. "Uterine Prolapse: From Antiquity to Today." *Obstetrics and Gynecology International,* 2012. Article ID 649459, doi:10.1155/2012/649459 Retrieved from: https://www.hindawi.com/journals/ogi/2012/649459/.

Dudzik, Kelly Norene. "Remember that Time Feminism Prolapsed My Uterus? Well I Fixed it!" *XOjane,* November 16, 2016. https://www.xojane.com/healthy/ multiple-types-of-kegels-for-a-prolapsed-uterus?page=6.

FDA website. "Pelvic Organ Prolapse." U.S. Food and Drug Admin. https://www.fda.gov/MedicalDevices/ ProductsandMedicalProcedures/Implantsand Prosthetics/UroGynSurgicalMesh/ucm262299.htm.

Friedman, Richard Elliot and Shawna Dolansky. *The Bible Now.* England, UK: Oxford University Press, 2011.

Newton, Piper. *And Then My Uterus Fell Out: A Memoir on life with Pelvic Organ Prolapse.* Flushing, NY: PRN, 2013.

ThatHappened website. "My Uterus is Falling Out." Reddit. https://www.reddit.com/r/thatHappened/comments/ 351zfr/my_uterus_is_falling_out/.

WebMD.com website. "How do I know if I'm in Menopause?" https://www.webmd.com/menopause/guide/understanding-menopause-symptoms#1.

Jouissance

Boseley, Sarah. "What is Female Genital Mutilation and where does it happen?" *The Guardian,* February 6, 2014. https:// www.theguardian.com/society/2014/feb/what-is-female-genital-mutilation-where-happen.

Bulletin of the World Health Organization. "Slow Progress in Ending Female Genital Mutilation," 2014. http://www. who.int/bulletin/volumes/92/1/14-020114/en/.

Knowing Jesus website. "Joy." https://bible.knowing-jesus. com/topics/Joy.

Knowing Jesus website. "Happiness." https://bible.knowing jesus.com/topics/Happiness.

Knowing Jesus website. "Joy and Happiness." https://bible. knowing-jesus.com/search?q=joy+and+happiness& translation=all.

Komisaruk, Barry and Wise, Nan. "Orgasms Better For Your Brain than Crossword Puzzles: Research Suggests." *The Huffington Post,* August 5, 2013. https://www.huffington post.com/2013/08/05/orgasms-good-for-you-study_ n_3708222.html.

Merriam Webster Dictionary website. Jouissance. https://www. merriam-webster.com/dictionary/jouissance

Price, Joan. "The 5 Health Benefits of Orgasms." *The Huffington Post,* September 24, 2013. https://www.huffington post.com/2013/09/24/health-benefits-of-orgasm_n_ 3956098.html.

Princesongs.org. "Do it All Night." *Dirty Mind* album, 1981. https://princesongs.org/2017/10/11/do-it-all-night/.

The Color Purple. Amblin Entertainment, 1985. http://www. imdb.com/title/tt0088939/.

Unicef.org website. "Female Genital Mutilation and Cutting." UNICEF Data: Monitoring the Situation of Children and Women. https://data.unicef.org/topic/child-protection/female-genital-mutilation-and-cutting/.

Proverbial Wisdom

Price-Thompson, Tracey. *Proverbs for the People.* New York: Kensington, 2003.

Proverbs of the World website. http://nepab.com/general/ proverbs.htm.

Schuster, Ellen. "Proverbs: A Path to Understanding Different Cultures." *Journal of Extension,* 36 (1), February 1998.

Crusin'

Ajayi, Luvvie. "Get Comfortable with being Uncomfortable." *TED Talk,* November 2017. https://www.ted.com/talks/luv vie_ajayi_get_comfortable_with_being_uncomfortable#t-640178.

End, Christian. "Fantasy vs. Reality: Response to Our Teams Performances." *Psychology Today,* September 28, 2014. https://www.psychologytoday.com/blog/the-roots-rooting/201409/fantasy-vs-reality-response-our-teams-performances.

Hinderaker, John. "Fantasy vs. Reality in November." *Power-line*, January 22, 2018. http://www.powerlineblog.com/archives/2018/01/fantasy-vs-reality-in-november.php.

Jones, Elka. "Reality vs. Fantasy in Occupational Portrayals on the Small Screen." *Occupational Quarterly Outlook,* Fall 2003. https://www.bls.gov/careeroutlook/2003/fall/art01.pdf.

Kamp, David. "Rethinking the American Dream." *Vanity Fair,* March 5, 2009. https://www.vanityfair.com/culture/2009/04/american-dream200904.

Kay, Michael. "Money Reality vs. Money Fantasy." *Forbes,* January 12, 2016. https://www.forbes.com/sites/.michaelkay/2016/01/.../money-reality-vs-money-fantasy

Simons, Keith. "Everquest: Blurring the Lines Between Reality and Fantasy." *Stanford.edu*, 2003. https://web.stanford.edu/group/htgg/sts145papers/ksimmons_2003_1.pdf.

Live Long and Prosper

"24," 2001-2010. https://www.imdb.com/title/tt0285331/

Avatar. 20th Century Fox. 2009. https://www.imdb.com/title/tt0499549/.

"Arsenio Hall Brings Back 'Things that make you go hmmm,'" 2011. *Access Hollywood Live.* http://www.accessonline.com/videos/access-hollywood-live-arsenio-hall-brings-back-things-that-make-you-go-hmmm-for-todays-biggest-scandals-28508/.

AVP: Alien vs. Predator. 20th Century Fox, 2004. http://www.imdb.com/title/tt0370263/.

Child Poverty. The National Center for Children in Poverty. Columbia University, 2018. http://www.nccp.org/topics/childpoverty.html.

District 9. TriStar Pictures. 2009. https://www.imdb.com/title/tt1136608/.

Elysium. TriStar Pictures. 2013. https://www.imdb.com/title/tt1535108/.

Higgins, Bill. "Hollywood's Flashback; Star Trek Showed TV's First Interracial Kiss in 1968." *Hollywood Reporter*, May 26, 2016. *Hunger Games.* Lions Gate, 2012. 2013. 2014. 2015. http://www.imdb.com/title/tt1392170/.

Independence Day: Resurgence. 20th Century Fox, 2016. https://www.imdb.com/title/tt1628841/.

In Time. New Regency Pictures. 2011. https://www.imdb.com/title/tt1637688/.

Nemetz, Dave. "Whoopi Goldberg Explains Why She Wanted to be on *Star Trek.*" *Yahoo Entertainment,* June 24, 2014. https://www.yahoo.com/entertainment/blogs/tv-news/exclusive-video-whoopi-goldberg-star-trek-213710247.html.

Pioneers of Television. Boettcher/Trinklein Productions, 2011. http://www.imdb.com/title/tt1821989/.

Robinson, Joanna. "8 Great Female Roles that were Originally Written for Men." *Vanity Fair,* June 7, 2015. https://www.vanityfair.com/hollywood/2015/06/female-characters-written-for-men.

Savage, Michael. "Richest One Percent on Target to Own Two Thirds of all Wealth by 2030." *The Guardian*, April 7, 2018. https://www.theguardian.com/business/2018/apr/07/global-inequality-tipping-point-2030.

Silverstein, Melissa. "Star Trek's Gender Problem." *The Huffington Post,* June 12, 2009. https://www.huffingtonpost.com/melissa-silverstein/star-treks-gender-problem_b_202066.html.

Star Trek. Paramount Television, 1966-1986. http://www.imdb.com/title/tt0060028/.

Star Trek: The Next Generation. Paramount Television, 1987-1994. http://www.imdb.com/title/tt0092455/.

Star Trek: Deep Space Nine. Paramount Television, 1993-1999. http://www.imdb.com/title/tt0092455/.

Star Trek Voyager. Paramount Television, 1995-2001. https://www.imdb.com/title/tt0112178/companycredits.

Star Trek Enterprise. Paramount Television, 2001-2005. http://www.imdb.com/title/tt0244365/.

Star Trek Into Darkness. Paramount Pictures, 2013. http://www.imdb.com/title/tt1408101/.

Star Trek. Paramount Pictures, 2009. http://www.imdb.com/title/tt0796366/.

Star Trek: Beyond. Paramount Pictures, 2016. http://www.imdb.com/title/tt2660888/.

Star Trek Database website. The Ferengi, 2018. http://www.startrek.com/database_article/ferengi.

State of Affairs, 2014-1015. NBC. https://www.imdb.com/title/tt3489236/.

Veep, 2012- . HBO. https://www.imdb.com/title/tt1759761/

The Walking Dead. AMC, 2010. http://www.imdb.com/title/tt1520211/.

Wallace, Rachel. "By the Numbers: A Look at the Gender Pay Gap." *The American Association of University Women,* 2014. https://www.aauw.org/research/the-simple-truth-about-the-gender-pay-gap/.

Wynonna Earp. SyFy Channel, 2016. http://www.imdb.com/title/tt4878326/.

God is Love

Bettelheim, Bruno. *The Uses of Enchantment: The Meaning and Importance of Fairy Tales*. Visaslia, CA: Vintage Press, 1976, 2010.

The New Testament. 1 John 4:8. Bible Gateway website. https://www.biblegateway.com/passage/?search=1+John+4%3A8

Pretty Woman. Touchstone Pictures, 1990. http://www.imdb.com/title/tt0100405/.

Sex and the City. HBO, 1998-2004. http://www.imdb.com/title/tt0159206/.

TV Fanatic website. Sex and the City. https://www.tvfanatic.com/quotes/its- because-women-really-just-want-to-be-rescued-there-it/.

Letting Go

Boomerang. Paramount Pictures, 1992. http://www.imdb.com/title/tt0103859/.

"Gender Distribution of Advanced Degrees in Humanities. Humanities Indicator." *American Academy of Arts and Sciences*, August 2017. https://humanitiesindicators.org/content/indicatordoc.aspx?i=47.

Miller, Donald. *Blue Like Jazz*. Nashville, TN: Thomas Nelson, 2003.

A Life Worth Living

"Racial/Ethnic Distribution of Advanced Degrees in Humanities. Humanities Indicator." *American Academy of Arts and Sciences*, August 2017. https://humanitiesindicators.org/content/indicatordoc.aspx?i=46.

Stein, Robert. *The Black Samaritan*. San Francisco, CA: Replica Books, October 2000.

Thagard, Paul. "What Makes Life Worth Living: Love, Work, and Play." *Psychology Today*, February 25, 2010.

Biography - Venise Berry

Venise Berry is the author of three national bestselling novels; *So Good, An African American Love Story* (Dutton Penguin, 1996), *All of Me, A Voluptuous Tale* (Dutton Penguin, 2000), and *Colored Sugar Water* (Dutton Penguin, 2002). She is currently finishing her fourth novel *Pockets of Sanity*.

Blackish, Black Jesus, and the First Black American President: Racialism and the Media is an examination of mediated images and messages concerning African American culture. It will be published by Peter Lang in 2019. Berry is also the co-editor of an anthology with Peter Lang, *Black Culture & Experience: Contemporary Issues* (2015). Two non-fiction books on black film were co-authored with her brother S. Torriano Berry a retired, associate professor in Film at Howard University; *The Historical Dictionary of African American Cinema* (Scarecrow Press, 2007 & 2nd Ed. 2015) and *The 50 Most Influential Black Films* (Citadel 2001).

Berry is published widely in creative and academic circles with numerous short stories, journal articles, and book chapters. Her research explores media, African Americans, and popular culture. Her first co-edited anthology, *Mediated Messages and African-American Culture: Contemporary Issues* (Sage, 1996) won the Meyers Center Award for the Study of Human Rights in North America in 1997.

She was honored in 2018 with an Iowa History Makers Award from the African American Museum in Cedar Rapids Iowa. In 2003, she received the Creative Contribution to Literature Award for *Colored Sugar Water* from the Zora Neale Hurston Society. *All of Me* received a 2001 Honor Book Award from the Black Caucus of the American Library Association.

Berry is an associate professor in Journalism and African American Studies at the University of Iowa in Iowa City. She received a bachelors degree (1977) in Journalism and a masters degree (1979) in Communication Studies from the University of Iowa. Her Ph.D. was awarded in 1989 in Radio. TV and Film at the University of Texas in Austin. Berry taught for 12 years at two historically black colleges, Texas Southern University and Huston-Tillotson College before returning to the University of Iowa.

She serves on the faculty each winter in the Solstice low-residency creative writing program at Pine Manor College in Chestnut Hill, MA and offers writing workshops every summer in the Iowa Summer Writing Festival. She has also conducted writing workshops with the Hurston/Wright Foundation and the Black Writers Conference and Reunion.

If you would like to talk about a workshop or a presentation event see contact information below.

Workshop/Presentation topics include:
  -Weight and Wellness: Challenging Myths
  -Success Strategies for the 21st Century
  -Racialism and the Media
  -Words That Set Us Free
  -Food for the Spirit

2121 Oakdale Circle
Coralville, IA 52241
(319) 337-7557
venise-berry@uiowa.edu